United States Government Accountability Office

Report to Congressional Requesters

I0448405

November 2013

GPS DISRUPTIONS

Efforts to Assess Risks to Critical Infrastructure and Coordinate Agency Actions Should Be Enhanced

GAO-14-15

GPS DISRUPTIONS

Efforts to Assess Risks to Critical Infrastructure and Coordinate Agency Actions Should Be Enhanced

GAO Highlights

Highlights of GAO-14-15, a report to congressional requesters

Why GAO Did This Study

GPS provides positioning, navigation, and timing data to users worldwide and is used extensively in many of the nation's 16 critical infrastructure sectors, such as communications and transportation. GPS is also a key component in many of the modern conveniences that people rely on or interact with daily. However, sectors' increasing dependency on GPS leaves them potentially vulnerable to disruptions. GAO was asked to review the effects of GPS disruptions on the nation's critical infrastructure. GAO examined (1) the extent to which DHS has assessed the risks and potential effects of GPS disruptions on critical infrastructure, (2) the extent to which DOT and DHS have developed backup strategies to mitigate GPS disruptions, and (3) what strategies, if any, selected critical infrastructure sectors employ to mitigate GPS disruptions and any remaining challenges. GAO reviewed documents, compared them to relevant federal guidance, and interviewed representatives and experts from federal and state governments, industry, and academia. The focus of this review was on civilian GPS uses within four critical infrastructure sectors.

What GAO Recommends

DHS should ensure that its GPS risk assessment approach is consistent with DHS guidance; develop a plan to measure the effectiveness of mitigation efforts; and DOT and DHS should improve collaboration. DHS concurred with the latter two recommendations but did not concur with the first. GAO continues to believe that improving the risk assessment approach will capitalize on progress DHS has made and will improve future efforts.

View GAO-14-15. For more information, contact Mark Goldstein at (202) 512-2834 or goldsteinm@gao.gov or Joseph Kirschbaum at (202) 512-9971 or kirschbaumj@gao.gov.

What GAO Found

To assess the risks and potential effects from disruptions in the Global Positioning System (GPS) on critical infrastructure, the Department of Homeland Security (DHS) published the GPS National Risk Estimate (NRE) in 2012. In doing so, DHS conducted a scenario-based risk assessment for four critical infrastructure sectors using subject matter experts from inside and outside of government. Risk assessments involve complex analysis, and conducting a risk assessment across multiple sectors with many unknowns and little data is challenging. DHS's risk management guidance can be used to help address such challenges. However, we found the NRE lacks key characteristics of risk assessments outlined in DHS's risk management guidance and, as a result, is incomplete and has limited usefulness to inform mitigation planning, priorities, and resource allocation. A plan to collect and assess additional data and subsequent efforts to ensure that the risk assessment is consistent with DHS guidance would contribute to more effective GPS risk management.

A 2004 presidential directive requires the Department of Transportation (DOT), in coordination with DHS, to develop backup capabilities to mitigate GPS disruptions, and the agencies have initiated a variety of efforts that contribute to fulfilling the directive. For example, DOT is researching GPS alternatives for aviation, and DHS began efforts on GPS interference detection and mitigation and is researching possibilities for a nationwide backup to GPS timing, which is used widely in critical infrastructure. However, due to resource constraints and other reasons, the agencies have made limited progress in meeting the directive, and many tasks remain incomplete, including identifying GPS backup requirements and determining suitability of backup capabilities. Furthermore, the agencies' efforts have been hampered by a lack of effective collaboration. In particular, DOT and DHS have not clearly defined their respective roles, responsibilities, and authorities or what outcomes would satisfy the presidential directive. Without clearly defining both roles and desired outcomes, DOT and DHS cannot ensure that they will satisfy mutual responsibilities. Implementing key elements of effective collaboration would allow the agencies to address many uncertainties regarding fulfillment of their presidential policy directive.

Selected critical infrastructure sectors employ various strategies to mitigate GPS disruptions. For example, some sectors can rely on timing capabilities from other sources of precise time in the event of GPS signal loss. However, both the NRE and stakeholders we interviewed raised concerns about the sufficiency of the sectors' mitigation strategies. Federal risk management guidance requires DHS to work with federal agencies and critical infrastructure sector partners to measure the nation's ability to reduce risks to critical infrastructure by using a process that includes metrics. We found that DHS has not measured the effectiveness of sector mitigation efforts to GPS disruptions and that, as a result, DHS cannot ensure that the sectors could sustain essential operations during GPS disruptions. The lack of agreed-upon metrics to measure the effectiveness of sector mitigation efforts hinders DHS's ability to objectively assess improvements, track progress, establish accountability, provide feedback mechanisms, or inform decision makers about the appropriateness of the mitigation activities.

_____ **United States Government Accountability Office**

Contents

Abbreviations

CS&C	Office of Cybersecurity and Communications
DHS	Department of Homeland Security
DOD	Department of Defense
DOE	Department of Energy
DOT	Department of Transportation
eLORAN	enhanced Long Range Navigation
FAA	Federal Aviation Administration
FCC	Federal Communications Commission
FOUO	For Official Use Only
GPS	Global Positioning System
HSPD-7	Homeland Security Presidential Directive 7
IDM	interference detection and mitigation
NASA	National Aeronautics and Space Administration
NAVCEN	U.S. Coast Guard Navigation Center
NCO	National Coordination Office for Space-Based Positioning, Navigation, and Timing
NextGen	Next Generation Air Transportation System
NIPP	National Infrastructure Protection Plan
NOAA	National Oceanic and Atmospheric Administration
NPPD	National Protection and Programs Directorate
NRE	National Risk Estimate
NSPD-39	National Security Presidential Directive 39
PNT	positioning, navigation, and timing
PPD-21	Presidential Policy Directive on Critical Infrastructure Security and Resilience
RITA	Research and Innovative Technology Administration
SCC	Sector Coordinating Council
SSA	Sector-Specific Agency
TSA	Transportation Security Administration

GAO U.S. GOVERNMENT ACCOUNTABILITY OFFICE

441 G St. N.W.
Washington, DC 20548

November 6, 2013

The Honorable Tom Coburn, M.D.
Ranking Member
Committee on Homeland Security and Governmental Affairs
United States Senate

The Honorable Michael T. McCaul
Chairman
Committee on Homeland Security
House of Representatives

The Honorable Susan M. Collins
United States Senate

The satellite-based Global Positioning System (GPS) provides positioning, navigation, and timing (PNT) data to users worldwide. GPS is used extensively in many infrastructure sectors, including most of the 16 sectors identified as critical to the nation's economy, security, and health—referred to as "critical infrastructure sectors."[1] Many of these critical infrastructure sectors have grown dependent on GPS technology as GPS-supported applications have become increasingly embedded in their operations. GPS is also a key component in many of the modern conveniences that people rely on or interact with daily. GPS receivers are in everything from cell phones and wristwatches to bulldozers, shipping containers, and automatic teller machines. However, interference from a variety of sources—such as space weather events or devices that intentionally block GPS signals—can disrupt GPS and affect its reliability.

The Department of Homeland Security (DHS) is responsible for coordinating a national effort to protect our critical infrastructure and

---

[1]According to presidential directive, there are 16 critical infrastructure sectors that are so vital to the United States that their incapacitation or destruction would have a debilitating effect on security, national economic security, national public health, or safety. The 16 sectors include chemical; commercial facilities; communications; critical manufacturing; dams; defense industrial base; emergency services; energy; financial services; food and agriculture; government facilities; healthcare and public health; information technology; nuclear reactors, materials, and waste; transportation systems; and water and wastewater systems. White House, *Critical Infrastructure Security and Resilience*, Presidential Policy Directive/PPD-21 (Feb. 12, 2013).

published a report in 2012 on the infrastructure risks from GPS disruptions. The Department of Transportation (DOT) serves as the lead civilian agency on GPS-related issues and represents all civilian agencies in issues related to GPS development, acquisition, management, and operations. The President directed DOT, in coordination with DHS, to develop, acquire, operate, and maintain backup PNT capabilities that can support critical civilian and commercial infrastructure within the United States during a GPS disruption.[2] The inability to mitigate the negative effects of a GPS disruption, especially a longer-term disruption, could potentially lead to loss of life or billions in economic losses.

You asked us to provide information on the risks and potential effects of GPS disruptions on the nation's critical infrastructure. This report examines (1) the extent to which DHS has assessed the risks of GPS disruptions and their potential effects on the nation's critical infrastructure, (2) the extent to which DOT and DHS have planned or developed backup capabilities or other strategies to mitigate the effects of GPS disruptions, and (3) what strategies, if any, selected critical infrastructure sectors employ to mitigate the effects of GPS disruptions, and any remaining challenges they face.

To address our objectives, we focused on civilian, as opposed to military, uses of GPS because the majority of GPS applications and users are civilian. We also focused on four critical infrastructure sectors—communications, energy, financial services, and transportation systems—because of their high degree of dependence on GPS and interdependence with other sectors, among other reasons. Similar to our prior reviews of DHS's risk assessments, we evaluated DHS's 2012 GPS risk assessment against established federal risk assessment criteria for critical infrastructure protection. We examined agency documentation on the efforts DOT and DHS have undertaken to plan or develop GPS backup capabilities, reviewed relevant federal policies and presidential directives, and compared the agencies' efforts to the requirements in these policies and directives. We compared DOT's and DHS's efforts

---

[2]White House, *U.S. Space-Based Positioning, Navigation, and Timing Policy*, National Security Presidential Directive/NSPD-39 (Dec. 15, 2004).

against our criteria on key elements of effective collaboration.[3] We also reviewed literature from academia and other GPS subject matter experts. Additionally, we contacted federal government officials from agencies involved in GPS governance—such as the Department of Defense (DOD), DOT, and DHS—and agencies involved in critical infrastructure protection for each of the four sectors we studied, such as the Department of Energy (DOE) and the Department of the Treasury. We also contacted state government officials through the U.S. States & Local Government Subcommittee of the Civil GPS Service Interface Committee, a forum established by DOT to exchange information about GPS with the civilian user community.[4] We contacted industry representatives for each of the four sectors we studied and various GPS subject matter experts, including members of the National Space-Based PNT Advisory Board (Advisory Board), a federal advisory committee that provides independent advice to the U.S. government on GPS matters.[5] In selecting GPS experts, we considered relevant published literature; their experience as reflected in publications, testimonies, positions held, and their biographies; and stakeholders' recommendations.

We conducted this performance audit from November 2012 through November 2013, in accordance with generally accepted government auditing standards. Those standards require that we plan and perform the audit to obtain sufficient, appropriate evidence to provide a reasonable basis for our findings and conclusions based on our audit objectives. We believe that the evidence obtained provides a reasonable basis for our findings and conclusions based on our audit objectives. A more detailed discussion of our objectives, scope, and methodology appears in appendix I.

---

[3]GAO, *Managing For Results: Key Considerations for Implementing Interagency Collaborative Mechanisms*, GAO-12-1022 (Washington, D.C.: Sept. 27, 2012); and *Results-Oriented Government: Practices That Can Help Enhance and Sustain Collaboration among Federal Agencies*, GAO-06-15 (Washington, D.C.: Oct. 21, 2005).

[4]Information on the Civil GPS Service Interface Committee is available at http://www.gps.gov/cgsic/, accessed September 25, 2013.

[5]Information on the Advisory Board is available at http://www.gps.gov/governance/advisory/, accessed September 25, 2013.

Background

The U.S. government has invested more than $5 billion since 2009 in GPS and provides GPS service free of direct charge to users worldwide. As shown in figure 1, GPS consists of the space segment, the ground-control segment, and the user segment. The U.S. Air Force develops, maintains, and operates the space and ground-control segments.

- The space segment consists of a constellation of satellites transmitting radio signals to users. The Air Force manages the constellation to ensure the availability of at least 24 GPS satellites 95 percent of the time.[6]

- The ground-control segment consists of a global network of ground facilities that track the GPS satellites, monitor their transmissions, perform analyses, and send commands and data to the constellation.

- The user segment consists of GPS receiver equipment, which receives the signals from the GPS satellites and uses the transmitted information to calculate the user's three-dimensional position and time.

---

[6]On May 15, 2013, the Air Force launched a new GPS satellite into orbit intended to improve GPS service worldwide. For more information on the Air Force's modernization of the system, see GAO, *Global Positioning System: Challenges in Sustaining and Upgrading Capabilities Persist*, GAO-10-636 (Washington, D.C.: Sept. 15, 2010).

Figure 1: GPS Operational Segments

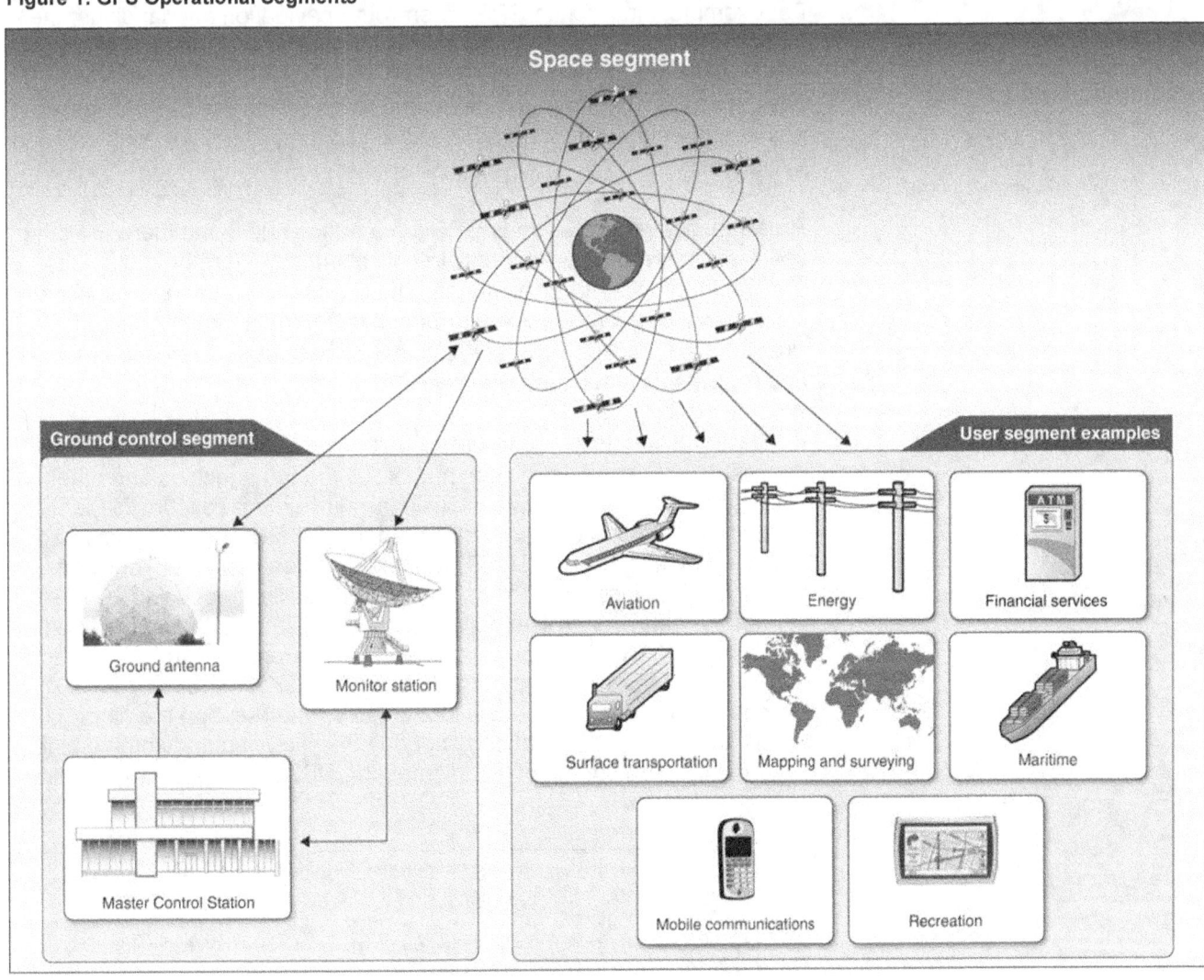

GPS is used extensively and in various ways in many critical infrastructure sectors for PNT information. For example, among other uses, the communications sector uses the GPS timing function to synchronize call handoffs in wireless communications. The energy sector's bulk power system uses GPS timing in a component that provides status measurements at frequent points in time. The financial services sector uses GPS timing to time stamp financial transactions, match trading orders, and synchronize financial computer systems. The transportation systems sector uses GPS for safe and efficient operations. For example, aircraft use GPS for en-route navigation and landings; the maritime industry uses GPS for navigation and as a safety and situational tool in high-traffic ports; commercial vehicles use GPS for positioning, navigation, and fleet management; and rail systems use GPS for asset management, tracking, and positive train control, which supports collision avoidance.[7]

Presidential directive assigns GPS governance roles, and there are other policies and directives that apply to critical infrastructure protection that are important for GPS governance. These policies and directives include: (1) National Security Presidential Directive 39, (2) Homeland Security Presidential Directive 7, (3) the National Infrastructure Protection Plan, and (4) Presidential Policy Directive 21.

- **National Security Presidential Directive 39 (NSPD-39)**.[8] NSPD-39 assigns governance roles to numerous federal agencies and other entities. In particular, within DOD, the Air Force is responsible for the overall development, acquisition, operation, security, and continued modernization of GPS. DOT serves as the lead civilian agency on GPS-related issues and has lead responsibility for developing requirements for civilian applications. DHS, through the U.S. Coast Guard's Navigation Center, provides user support to the civilian, non-aviation GPS community. Additionally, NSPD-39 requires that DOT, in coordination with DHS, develop, acquire, operate, and maintain backup capabilities that can support critical civilian and commercial infrastructure during a GPS disruption.[9] NSPD-39 also assigns DHS

---

[7]We have reported on the use of GPS in the transportation systems sector. See GAO, *Federal Vehicle Fleets: Adopting Leading Practices Could Improve Management*, GAO-13-659 (Washington, D.C.: July 31, 2013); and GAO, *Positive Train Control: Additional Authorities Could Benefit Implementation*, GAO-13-720 (Washington, D.C.: Aug. 16, 2013).

[8]Issued in December 2004, NSPD-39 is also known as the 2004 U.S. Space-Based Positioning, Navigation, and Timing Policy. "Space-based PNT" refers to GPS, GPS augmentations, and other global navigation satellite systems.

[9]DOT and DHS jointly recommended pursuing the designation of the enhanced Long Range Navigation system (eLORAN), an upgraded version of the ground-based navigation system LORAN-C, as a national backup to GPS, and in 2008, DHS formally committed to implementing eLORAN. However, for various reasons LORAN-C was decommissioned in 2010, terminating eLORAN plans. Although the fiscal year 2009 President's Budget Proposal included funding for DHS to implement eLORAN, Congress did not provide an appropriation for this purpose.

(in coordination with other agencies) the responsibility to identify, locate, and attribute any interference within the United States that adversely affects GPS use and to develop a central repository and database for reports of domestic and international interference to GPS civilian services. NSPD-39 also directed the federal government to improve the performance of space-based PNT services, including by developing more robust resistance to interference for national security purposes, homeland security, and civilian, commercial, and scientific users worldwide. Furthermore, NSPD-39 assigns the Department of Commerce and the Federal Communications Commission (FCC) responsibility for mitigating electronic interference with U.S. space-based PNT services within the United States.[10] NSPD-39 also established a National Executive Committee for Space-Based PNT (National Executive Committee), chaired jointly by DOD and DOT, to coordinate GPS-related matters across federal agencies. The National Coordination Office for Space-Based PNT (NCO) houses the permanent staff of the National Executive Committee and provides day-to-day support for the committee's activities. Among other things, the National Executive Committee issued a 5-year plan for space-based PNT that recommends that DHS institute a risk management approach to assess threats, vulnerabilities, and potential consequences to interference to GPS signals and examine the best opportunities to mitigate those risks.[11] See figure 2 for the national space-based PNT organization structure.

---

[10]The President's 2010 National Space Policy also refers to GPS and critical infrastructure and states that the United States shall invest in domestic capabilities and support international activities to detect, mitigate, and increase resiliency to harmful interference to GPS, and identify and implement, as necessary and appropriate, redundant and backup systems or approaches for critical infrastructure, key resources, and mission-essential functions. White House, *National Space Policy of the United States of America*, Presidential Policy Directive/PPD-4 (June 28, 2010).

[11]Space-Based Positioning, Navigation and Timing National Executive Committee, *National Five-Year Plan for Space-Based PNT for Fiscal Years 2009-2013*, signed June 2009.

Figure 2: National Space-Based Positioning, Navigation, and Timing (PNT) Organization Chart

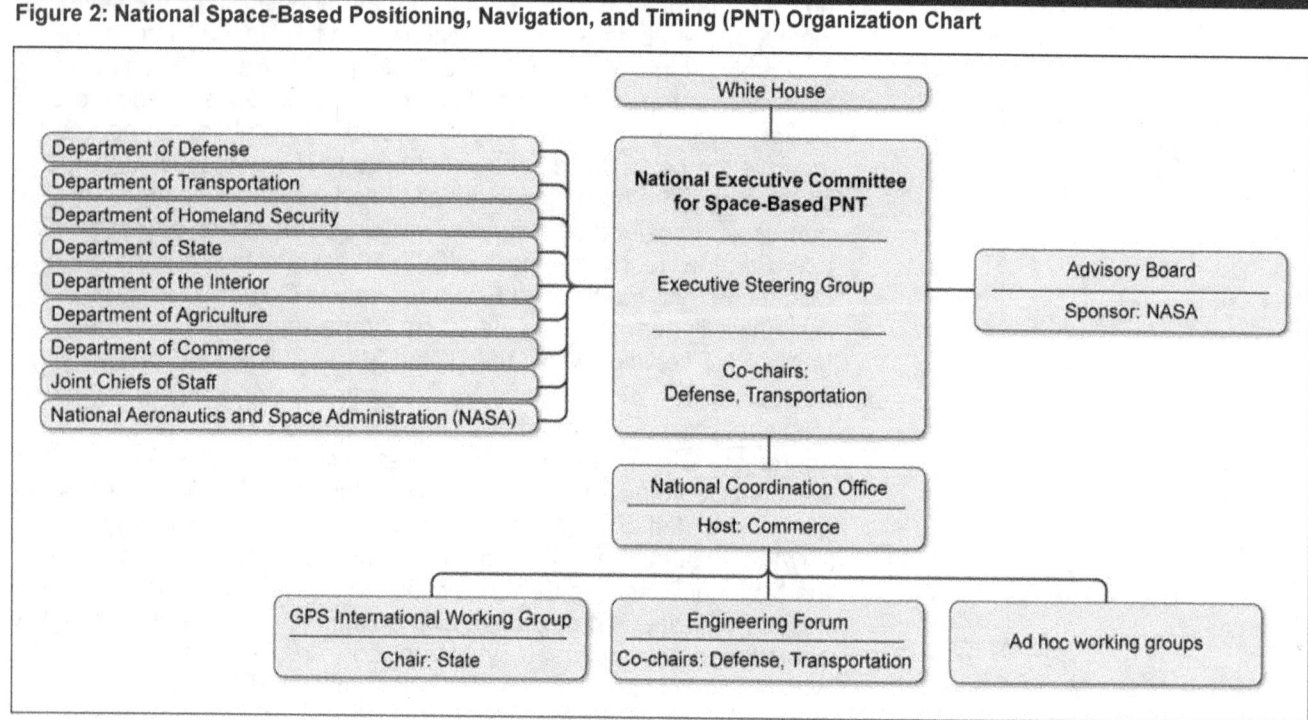

Source: GAO presentation of National Executive Committee for Space-Based PNT information.

- **Homeland Security Presidential Directive 7 (HSPD-7)**.[12] Issued in 2003, the purpose of HSPD-7 was to establish a national policy for federal departments and agencies to identify, prioritize, and protect critical infrastructure and key resources. HSPD-7 designated DHS as the agency responsible for coordinating the nation's efforts to protect critical infrastructure. DHS was directed to coordinate protection activities for each critical infrastructure sector through designated Sector-Specific Agencies (SSA). In accordance with applicable laws or regulations, DHS and the SSAs were directed to collaborate with appropriate private sector entities and continue to encourage the development of information sharing and analysis mechanisms to identify, prioritize, and coordinate the protection of critical infrastructure and key resources.

---

[12]White House, *Critical Infrastructure Identification, Prioritization, and Protection,* Homeland Security Presidential Directive/HSPD-7 (Dec. 17, 2003).

GAO-14-15 Impact of GPS Disruptions

- **National Infrastructure Protection Plan (NIPP).**[13] In 2006, DHS addressed the requirements of HSPD-7 by issuing the first NIPP, which DHS updated in 2009. The NIPP provides an overarching approach for integrating the nation's many critical infrastructure protection initiatives. The cornerstone of the NIPP is its risk management framework, which defines roles and responsibilities for DHS, the SSAs, and other federal, state, regional, local, and private sector partners.[14] Assessing risks is part of this framework, and the NIPP specifies core criteria for risk assessments. The NIPP specifically identifies GPS as a system that supports or enables critical functions in critical infrastructure sectors.

- **Presidential Policy Directive 21 (PPD-21).**[15] Issued in February 2013, PPD-21 supersedes HSPD-7 and states that critical infrastructure must be secure and able to withstand and rapidly recover from all hazards.[16] The directive refines and clarifies the critical infrastructure-related functions, roles, and responsibilities across the federal government, as well as aims to enhance overall coordination and collaboration. PPD-21 directs DHS to conduct comprehensive assessments of the vulnerabilities of the nation's critical infrastructure in coordination with the SSAs and in collaboration with critical infrastructure owners and operators. Executive Order 13636 was also issued in February 2013 to improve critical infrastructure cybersecurity.[17] According to DHS, implementation of the executive order and PPD-21 includes updating the NIPP by October 2013.[18]

---

[13]DHS, *National Infrastructure Protection Plan: Partnering to Enhance Protection and Resiliency* (2009).

[14]Sector partners are public and private critical infrastructure owners and operators.

[15]White House, *Critical Infrastructure Security and Resilience*, Presidential Policy Directive/PPD-21 (Feb. 12, 2013).

[16]According to DHS, while PPD-21 supersedes HSPD-7, any plans developed pursuant to HSPD-7 remain in effect until specifically revoked or superseded, including the NIPP.

[17]Improving Critical Infrastructure Cybersecurity, Exec. Order No. 13636, 78 Fed. Reg. 11737 (Feb. 19, 2013).

[18]In November 2013, a DHS official told us that the update to the 2009 NIPP was not released in October 2013 due to the federal government shutdown.

Disruption of the GPS signal can come from a variety of sources, including radio emissions in nearby bands, jamming, spoofing, and naturally occurring space weather.[19]

- Spectrum encroachment from radio emissions in nearby bands can cause interference to the GPS signal when the stronger radio signals overpower the relatively weak GPS signals from space.[20] Additionally, according to FCC, some GPS receivers are purposefully designed to receive as much energy as possible from GPS satellites, which makes the receivers vulnerable to interference from operations in nearby bands. With this type of interference, GPS devices pick up the stronger radio signals and become ineffective.

- Jamming devices are radio frequency transmitters that intentionally block, jam, or interfere with lawful communications, such as GPS signals.

- Spoofing involves the replacement of a true satellite signal with a manipulated signal, whereby the user may not realize they are using an incorrect GPS signal and may continue to rely on it. Articles and lab experiments have illustrated potential for harm in the bulk power system, maritime navigation, financial markets, and mobile communications, among other areas.

- Space weather can also cause interference to GPS signals. For example, during solar flare eruptions, the sun produces radio waves that can interfere with a broad frequency range, including those frequencies used by GPS.[21]

---

[19]Intentional interference with GPS signals, including jamming and spoofing GPS signals, is prohibited under 47 U.S.C. § 333. See, also, 47 U.S.C. § 302a(b) and 47 U.S.C. § 301.

[20]Radio frequency spectrum is the part of the natural spectrum of electromagnetic radiation lying between the frequency limits of 3 kilohertz and 300 gigahertz. Radio frequencies are grouped into bands.

[21]In addition to solar flare eruptions, GPS can be affected by other space weather events such as solar radiation storms, geomagnetic storms, and ionospheric interference.

GAO-14-15 Impact of GPS Disruptions

DHS Completed a Risk Assessment for GPS, but It Is Incomplete and Does Not Fully Conform to Guidance

DHS Issued a GPS National Risk Estimate

In September 2011, to fulfill the National Executive Committee's request for a comprehensive assessment of civilian GPS risks, DHS issued the National Risk Estimate (NRE) to the NCO; DHS officials said the final NRE was published in November 2012 with minor revisions.[22] According to DHS officials, the NRE is modeled after other risk estimates and efforts in the intelligence community. In developing the NRE, DHS conducted a scenario-based risk assessment for critical infrastructure using subject matter experts from inside and outside government. The NRE focuses on 4 of the 16 critical infrastructure sectors: communications, emergency services, energy, and transportation systems.[23] According to DHS officials, they chose these 4 sectors because they use GPS to support or fulfill their core missions and because they provide an appropriate cross-section of risks and potential impacts that could apply broadly to other sectors. The NRE considers three types of GPS disruption scenarios: (1) naturally occurring disruptions, such as space weather events; (2) unintentional disruptions, such as radio frequency signals interfering with GPS signals; and (3) intentional disruptions, such as jamming or spoofing. DHS solicited information from federal and private sector stakeholders and held several workshops on various risk scenarios with the subject matter experts, including one on the overall likelihood of

---

[22]DHS, *National Risk Estimate: Risks to U.S. Critical Infrastructure From Global Positioning System Disruptions*. Since the NRE is designated "For Official Use Only," it was released in November 2012 to only certain individuals who hold the proper clearance and access approval for the information. The National Executive Committee requested that DHS conduct a risk and mitigation study of GPS disruptions. DHS chose to conduct the risk assessment (the NRE), and to commission a separate mitigation study. See, Homeland Security Systems Engineering and Development Institute, *GPS Critical Infrastructure Risk Mitigation Techniques* (Sept. 28, 2011).

[23]At the time the NRE was conducted, there were 18 critical infrastructure sectors. Also at that time, the financial services sector was called the banking and finance sector.

occurrence of the risk scenarios. DHS also held sector-specific workshops on the consequences of GPS disruptions and alternative futures for each sector based on varying degrees of community attention to these security challenges.[24] DHS used alternative futures to consider the risk outlook over the next 20 years. According to DHS, the process of developing the NRE helped clarify aspects of critical infrastructure dependence on GPS and vulnerability to interference or an outage that were previously uncertain. Specifically, DHS officials told us that the NRE helped them understand the significance of the wide usage of GPS timing in systems throughout the nation's critical infrastructure. According to DHS, through the NRE workshops and the exchange of ideas, sector representatives also developed greater awareness of risks.

The NRE Did Not Fully Follow Risk Assessment Guidance or Fully Assess GPS Risks

Risk assessments, such as the NRE, involve complex analysis; conducting a risk assessment across multiple sectors of systems with many unknowns and little data is particularly challenging. The NIPP specifies core criteria for risk assessments and provides a framework for managing risk among the nation's critical infrastructure sectors. Aspects of DHS's NRE are consistent with the NIPP, such as the use of scenarios and subject matter experts and considering both the present and future level of risk. However, the NRE lacks key characteristics of risk assessments as outlined in the NIPP, and the NRE has not been widely used to inform risk mitigation priorities. The lack of an overall DHS plan and time frame to collect relevant threat, vulnerability, and consequence data and to develop a risk assessment approach more consistent with the NIPP could continue to hinder the ability of federal and private leaders to manage the risks associated with GPS disruptions.

The NIPP states that risk assessment is at the core of critical infrastructure protection and that it can be used to help address the associated challenges through its framework for assessing risk. The NIPP identifies the essential characteristics of a good risk assessment and calls for risk assessments to be (1) complete, (2) reproducible, (3) defensible, and (4) documented so that results can contribute to cross-sector risk comparisons for supporting investment, planning, and resource prioritization decisions. Our review of these NIPP characteristics with respect to the NRE follows.

---

[24]Alternative futures are plausible alternative views about how the future may develop.

- **Complete**. According to the NIPP, to be complete, the methodology should assess threat, vulnerability, and consequence for every defined risk scenario. We found the NRE examines these three key elements of a risk assessment but does not fully conform to the NIPP because, as described below, the NRE does not consider all relevant threats or assess the vulnerabilities of each sector reviewed, and the consequence assessment is incomplete because it fails to estimate the potential losses. In addition, the NRE considers just four critical infrastructure sectors. DHS officials acknowledged that their assessment was in some respects limited because they chose not to include all sectors due to resources and time constraints.[25] For example, DHS planning documents state that they had originally planned to include the banking and finance sector, but DHS officials told us that they dropped it when they could not identify the subject matter experts necessary to complete a risk analysis. The NIPP highlighted the importance of the banking and finance sector as a high-risk critical infrastructure sector, noted that nearly all sectors share relationships with banking and finance, and stated that banking and finance relies on GPS as its primary timing source.

- **Reproducible**. According to the NIPP, the methodology must produce comparable, repeatable results, and minimize the use of subjective judgments, leaving policy and value judgments to be applied by decision makers. We found the NRE does not conform to the NIPP because it is based entirely on subjective judgments of panelists and is not reproducible. Three subject matter experts we interviewed told us they were skeptical about the quality of the panel deliberations and characterized the member judgments as "educated guesses." Moreover, if different panelists were chosen, the results might have been different.

- **Defensible**. According to the NIPP, the methodology should be logical, make appropriate use of professional disciplines, and be free of significant errors and omissions. Uncertainty of estimates and level of confidence should be communicated. The NRE addresses some of these standards, including identifying various uncertainties related to its estimates. However, it is unclear that DHS made appropriate use of professional disciplines. Given the lack of data, subject matter

---

[25]DHS officials stated that they had to limit their scope when the National Executive Committee shortened the time for their study from 18 months to 12 months. However, the documentation provided by the NCO supports that the request was for 12 months.

experts were called upon to inform DHS's statistical modeling. DHS officials told us that they depended on the SSAs to suggest subject matter experts and used a consultant to identify subject matter experts beyond the SSAs' suggestions. However, industry representatives we interviewed questioned whether the panels had sufficiently broad expertise to capture the full scope of GPS vulnerabilities within sectors. For example, energy sector industry representatives told us that the energy sector panel experts only covered certain aspects of the electricity industry, not the entire energy sector. DHS officials told us that that at times the SSAs had difficulty suggesting subject matter experts. According to one official, it was difficult to find people within the various sectors who understood how GPS was embedded in their operations; he noted that sometimes it took 20 to 30 telephone calls in a given sector to locate an individual well-versed on the subject. However, decisions on expert selection are not documented in the NRE, meaning others cannot reasonably review and reproduce the NRE's efforts. In addition, we found the NRE's calculations of risk are not sufficiently transparent to assess whether the risk estimates are defensible and free of significant error. For example, the NRE's documentation is insufficiently transparent to support its determination that unintentional interference is a high risk for all four selected sectors where likelihood is high, but the consequences are deemed to be fairly low for three of the four sectors. Further, in the energy sector, a sophisticated, coordinated, continuous pinpointed spoofing attack against multiple targets is rated as having greater consequences than the other scenarios, yet due to its low estimated likelihood, is rated as having the lowest risk for energy scenarios. Without adequate explanation or presentation of the underlying data, the NRE lacks the transparency to verify that the estimate is defensible and free of significant error. Similarly, scenarios with the greatest uncertainty are rated as having the highest risk without sufficient data for an independent reviewer to verify. We requested additional documentation of these estimates, but DHS did not provide it.

- **Documented**. According to the NIPP, the assumptions and methodology used to generate the risk assessment must be clearly documented. The NRE did include elements that were consistent with the NIPP, such as describing the NRE's underlying analytic assumptions, its various workshops on likelihood and consequences, and its use of subject matter experts and a statistical simulation model to overcome limited data. Nonetheless, we found that overall, the NRE does not conform to this guideline because, as previously noted, it does not document how the subject matter experts, who were identified as inside and outside government, were selected. Absent reliable data, the NRE depends on the reliability of the expert panels. This and other documentation issues, such as not fully reporting the underlying data supporting the risk calculations, also affect the NRE's reproducibility and defensibility.

Furthermore, the NIPP states that risk is a function of three components—threat, vulnerability, and consequence—and a risk assessment approach must assess each component for every defined risk scenario. We found that there are factors in the NRE's analysis that specifically undermined the validity of the three components of a risk assessment, as follows.

- **Threat**. According to the NIPP, risk assessments should estimate an intentional threat as the likelihood that an adversary would attempt a given attack method against a target, and for other hazards, threat is generally estimated as the likelihood that a hazard will manifest itself. To complete the NRE, DHS issued data calls and held a workshop on the overall likelihood of GPS disruptions. Nonetheless, the NRE overall does not conform to the NIPP because the NRE neither uses its threat assessment to inform its threat-likelihood rankings, nor considers all relevant threats. In a separate classified annex, the NRE considers the threat likelihood of a range of GPS disruptions, which follows NIPP guidance to consider terrorist capability and intent. However, DHS officials told us that this threat information was not used for the NRE. DHS officials stated that the DHS Office of Intelligence and Analysis had not provided a draft of the threat annex in time for the May 6, 2011, scenario likelihood workshop, so the annex could not inform the ranking of the scenario likelihoods. The NIPP also requires an all-hazards approach for risk assessment. DHS officials told us that their selection of GPS disruption scenarios was based on discussions with subject matter experts. However, it is unclear how the threats for the risk scenarios were selected. For instance, while the NRE cites the threat of spectrum encroachment, which involves the potential for interference from new communication services near GPS frequencies, and considers alternative futures scenarios based in part on how potential spectrum encroachment is managed, it is not clear why the risk scenarios did not include the risk of interference to GPS receivers from operations in other frequency bands.[26] DHS officials told us that while the spectrum encroachment issue was relevant and a topic of discussion with subject matter experts during the NRE's development, it was outside the scope of what the NRE sought to assess because it stems from policy making rather than a threat from potential adversaries.

- **Vulnerability**. The vulnerability assessment in the NRE does not meet the criteria in the NIPP because it does not identify vulnerabilities specific to the sector nor the GPS dependencies of the sectors' key systems. Instead, the NRE assessed general vulnerabilities that did not consider specific sectors or the key systems used by those sectors. Without such a sector-specific assessment, the NRE does not adequately identify critical infrastructure systems' vulnerabilities and critical dependencies, nor develop estimates of the likelihood that an attack or hazard could cause harm. The NRE states that DHS was constrained in conducting unique vulnerability assessments for each of the four sectors because of limited data and key uncertainties. The NRE acknowledges that this constraint is a limitation of the report and that a likelihood workshop was used to estimate a combined threat and vulnerability assessment.

---

[26]As the NRE notes, over the past decade, GPS has faced threats from other systems operating in the same or adjacent radio frequency bandwidth or spectrum. There are two recent examples of industry seeking to repurpose spectrum to accommodate new technologies: (1) In 2000, Ultra Wide Band was proposed as a form of wireless communications technology that fused wireless, radar, and positioning technologies. Testing showed that Ultra Wide Band could disrupt certain GPS services, and development and deployment did not proceed. For more information, see Ming Luo, et al, *Testing and Research on Interference to GPS from UWB Transmitters* (Proceedings of the 14th International Technical Meeting of the Satellite Division of The Institute of Navigation, 2001). (2) In 2010, LightSquared Subsidiary LLC sought FCC approval to develop a nationwide, commercial wireless broadband network that would employ both terrestrial and satellite-based technology. According to FCC, in 2011, FCC issued an order conditioning LightSquared's commencement of commercial operations on LightSquared's completion of a process resolving interference concerns related to GPS; that process has not been completed. Moreover, subsequent testing has shown that the proposed commercial operations could potentially cause interference to certain GPS services. In February 2012, FCC sought comment on whether to vacate LightSquared's conditional authorization to commence commercial operations. *International Bureau Invites Comment on NTIA Letter Regarding Lightsquared Conditional Waiver*, 27 FCC Rcd. 1596 (Feb.15, 2012). As of August 2013, FCC had not issued a final order on the matter. For more information, see National Space-Based Positioning, Navigation, and Timing Systems Engineering Forum, *Assessment of Lightsquared Terrestrial Broadband System Effects on GPS Receivers and GPS-dependent Applications* (June 2011).

- **Consequence**. The NIPP states that at a minimum, consequences should focus on the two most fundamental components—human consequences and the most relevant direct economic consequences. For the NRE, DHS held sector-specific workshops on the consequences of GPS disruptions and projected a risk outlook over the next 20 years. However, the NRE focuses on assessing the potential impacts on sector functions, but does not assess how disruptions in those sector functions could affect the economy or safety of life. Without more specific analysis of the consequences, the overall risks from GPS disruptions cannot be calculated or compared across all sectors. DHS officials acknowledged that this was an area for improvement. The NRE also discusses sector interdependencies at a high level, but DHS did not survey the potential economic or safety-of-life consequences of these interdependencies.

The NIPP and other DHS guidance states that risk assessments are to be used to inform planning and priorities; however, we found the NRE has not been widely used. In particular, in addition to the NIPP guidance, the DHS strategic plan and risk management framework state that risk assessments should be used to inform and prioritize risk mitigation. The NRE states that it is to be used to inform executive-level decisions. The NCO told us that the NRE's intended use was to help inform senior government officials about the risks posed to the nation's critical infrastructure sectors by relying upon the GPS signal. NCO officials stated that they and the National Executive Committee, which requested the study, were satisfied with the NRE. The NRE has also been distributed to other federal agencies. One DHS component, the Office of Cybersecurity and Communications, told us that the NRE had been helpful in understanding some of the threats, especially to timing, but officials from another component, the Transportation Security Administration (TSA), told us that they are not using the NRE. For example, TSA officials said they found the NRE to be very general and did not see the relevance to TSA. Officials from two other agencies, the Departments of Defense and Energy, told us that the NRE was not helpful. Subject matter experts we contacted, some of whom participated in the NRE, expressed their concerns about the validity of the NRE, and one noted that industry does not have access to the final NRE because it is designated "For Official Use Only" (FOUO). DHS officials told us that in 2013, DHS began using the NRE to inform the planning and prioritization of initial steps to raise awareness of GPS disruptions. For example, among other things, they uploaded the NRE to a homeland security information-sharing portal to share with sector partners, and they told us that they have recently begun using the NRE for outreach to raise sector awareness but, as to specific guidance, they could only provide an example of brief correspondence encouraging sectors to identify their specific sources for PNT data. It has been 2 years since the NRE was issued and these preliminary steps do not rise to the level of a plan and a time frame to address how the considerable data gaps across 16 critical infrastructure sectors are to be closed.

In response to the National Executive Committee's request for a risk and mitigation assessment, DHS commissioned a separate study that was performed concurrently with the NRE. According to the NIPP, mitigation approaches should use the risk assessment's results to establish priorities and determine those actions that could provide the greatest risk mitigation benefits and inform planning and resource decisions. The mitigation report does not use the risk assessment's results of the NRE and instead, focused on generic mitigation issues and technologies.[27] As a result, it is unclear whether the pursuit of the mitigation report's recommendations would address the highest risks of GPS disruption to critical infrastructure.

DHS officials acknowledged the data and methodological limitations of the NRE, but stated that they have no plans to conduct another NRE on GPS because of resource constraints. The lack of an overall DHS plan and time frame to collect relevant data, periodically review the readiness of data to conduct a more robust risk assessment, and develop a risk assessment approach more consistent with the NIPP could continue to hinder the ability of federal and private leaders to manage the risks associated with GPS disruptions. Based on our review, opportunities exist for DHS to develop an enhanced risk assessment. For example, recent assessments performed by the private sector continue to report that the risk associated with GPS disruptions are a growing concern and that there are potential economic consequences. By considering this additional threat, vulnerability, and consequence information, DHS would be better positioned to employ a GPS risk assessment approach consistent with the NIPP. Furthermore, as previously mentioned, the National Executive Committee's 5-year plan for 2009-2013 also recommends that DHS institute a risk management approach to assessing threats, vulnerabilities, and potential consequences to

---

[27]Homeland Security Systems Engineering and Development Institute, *GPS Critical Infrastructure Risk Mitigation Technologies* (Sept. 28, 2011).

interference to GPS signals and examine the best opportunities to mitigate those risks.[28] Because of the shortcomings we found in the NRE, we do not believe that DHS has instituted an adequate risk management approach to address the risks associated with GPS interference.

DOT and DHS Have Initiated Mitigation Efforts, but Have Not Met All Requirements

DOT and DHS Are Required to Develop Backup Capabilities to Mitigate GPS Disruptions but Have Made Limited Progress

According to a presidential directive, DOT, in coordination with DHS, is required to develop, acquire, operate, and maintain backup capabilities that can support critical civilian and commercial infrastructure in the event of a GPS disruption.[29] NSPD-39 also assigns DHS (in coordination with other agencies) the responsibility to identify, locate, and attribute any interference that adversely affects GPS use and to develop a central repository and database for reports of domestic and international interference. DOT and DHS have initiated a variety of ongoing mitigation efforts that contribute to fulfilling their presidential directive, such as (1) developing plans and strategies for the nation's PNT architecture, (2) researching GPS alternatives for aviation, (3) developing plans and strategies for GPS interference detection, (4) researching possibilities for a nationwide timing backup, and (5) conducting other studies.

- **Developing plans and strategies for the nation's PNT architecture.** As a precursor to providing GPS backup capabilities per NSPD-39, DOT, in conjunction with DOD and with participation from 31 government agencies, including DHS, developed a national PNT architecture report and implementation plan to help guide the federal government's PNT investment decisions. Issued in 2008, the National PNT Architecture report documented the nation's current mix of "ad

---

[28]Space-Based Positioning, Navigation and Timing National Executive Committee, *National Five-Year Plan for Space-Based Positioning, Navigation and Timing, Fiscal years 2009-2013.*

[29]White House, *U.S. Space-Based Positioning, Navigation, and Timing Policy,* National Security Presidential Directive/NSPD-39 (Dec. 15, 2004).

hoc" PNT sources and identified a number of capability gaps.[30] To address these gaps, the report recommended that the nation transition to a "greater common denominator" strategy, where the PNT needs of many users are efficiently met through commonly available solutions, rather than numerous, individual systems. Additionally, the report acknowledged that GPS is the cornerstone of the nation's PNT capabilities and made a number of recommendations that would ensure continued availability of PNT service during GPS disruptions through, for example, the ability to provide PNT from alternative sources when a primary source is not available. The National PNT Architecture implementation plan, released in 2010, identified the tasks federal agencies would need to take to implement the report's recommendations.[31]

- **Researching GPS alternatives for aviation**. Through the Federal Aviation Administration's (FAA) Alternative PNT initiative, DOT is researching potential GPS backup solutions for the Next Generation Air Transportation System (NextGen).[32] To meet NextGen's navigation and performance requirements, GPS will be the primary navigation aid for aircraft. According to FAA officials, the legacy navigation systems currently used by aircraft during GPS disruptions are not capable of supporting new NextGen capabilities. As a result, FAA is conducting feasibility studies and analysis on three potential systems that can be used as a GPS backup for NextGen and, according to FAA officials, expects to make a decision by 2016.

- **Developing plans and strategies for GPS interference detection**. In 2007, DHS began efforts on GPS interference detection and mitigation (IDM) to improve the federal government's ability to detect, locate, and mitigate sources of GPS interference. Among DHS's planned activities were developing a central repository for GPS

---

[30]DOD, *National Positioning, Navigation, and Timing Architecture Study Final Report* (Sept. 2008).

[31]DOT and DOD, *National Positioning, Navigation, and Timing Architecture Implementation Plan* (Apr. 2010).

[32]NextGen is an initiative to modernize the nation's air traffic control system. For more information on NextGen, see GAO, *NextGen Air Transportation System: FAA Has Made Progress in Midterm Implementation, but Ongoing Challenges Limit Expected Benefits*, GAO-13-264 (Washington, D.C.: Apr. 8, 2013).

interference reports, and identifying GPS backup-system requirements and determining suitability of backup capabilities.[33]

- **Researching possibilities for a nationwide timing backup**. According to DHS officials, in 2012 the Coast Guard entered into a research agreement with a technology company to test alternative, non-space-based sources of precise time. Additionally, according to DHS officials, in late 2012 the National Institute of Standards and Technology began researching the possibility of using the nation's fiber networks as an alternative, non-space-based source of precise time. Both research efforts are ongoing.

- **Conducting other studies**. DHS has conducted or commissioned other studies related to GPS mitigation. For example, in 2009, DHS surveyed federal agencies to better understand their GPS capabilities, requirements, and backup systems. However, not all SSAs responded to DHS's requests for information. As previously mentioned, DHS also commissioned a study of GPS risk mitigation techniques, which was conducted concurrently with the NRE and issued in 2011. Among other things, the study described actions that GPS users can take to improve the resiliency of their GPS receivers against jamming and spoofing and recommended that federal regulators of critical infrastructure ensure that the infrastructure they regulate possesses sufficient resiliency to operate without GPS timing.[34] According to DHS officials, DHS continues to examine the study's findings and recommendations, although specific actions remain unbudgeted. In commenting on a draft of this report, DHS noted that it also awarded funding in May 2013 to develop technologies to detect and localize sources of GPS disruptions, among other things, and in July 2013, commissioned a study to assess potential sector-specific and cross-sector threat mitigation technologies, among other things, for the communications sector and electricity subsector of the energy sector.

Although DOT and DHS have taken the above initiatives, they have made limited progress implementing their plans to develop, acquire, operate,

---

[33]DHS officials highlighted that while DHS leads IDM efforts, GPS-provided PNT data are transported across spectrum regulated for non-federal-government use by FCC and that it is FCC that resolves complaints, investigates, and takes or recommends enforcement action against radio frequency interference.

[34]Homeland Security Systems Engineering and Development Institute, *GPS Critical Infrastructure Risk Mitigation Techniques* (Sept. 28, 2011).

and maintain backup capabilities and, overall, the requirements of NSPD-39 remain unfulfilled. For example, with respect to DOT efforts, little progress has been made on the tasks outlined in the National PNT Architecture implementation plan since its issuance 3 years ago. DOT officials cited a variety of reasons why additional progress has not been made, including resource constraints, uncertainty, and competing priorities. In particular, DOT assigned lead responsibility for PNT to the Research and Innovative Technology Administration (RITA), yet RITA's Office of PNT and Spectrum Management has three full-time staff members, one of whom works on the National PNT Architecture implementation plan in addition to other responsibilities. One senior DOT official involved in GPS management also stated that, organizationally, another key issue was uncertainty surrounding which federal agencies would take responsibility for ensuring the plan was implemented and for funding the various tasks and programs. According to this official, the implementation plan did not get optimal support from federal agencies that were assigned tasks because these agencies did not have resources to devote to completing those tasks. In addition, DOT officials said little progress was made on the implementation plan because immediately after its issuance in 2010, DOT staff with GPS expertise shifted their focus to proceedings surrounding a wireless broadband network proposal by a company called Lightsquared—a proposal which government officials, industry representatives, and GPS experts demonstrated could cause significant GPS interference.[35] However, DOT officials stated that information supporting the implementation plan has been incorporated into the most recent *Federal Radionavigation Plan*.[36]

Similarly, DHS has completed few IDM activities, though the agency has taken some steps. For example, DHS established an incident portal to serve as a central repository for all agencies reporting incidents of GPS interference and developed draft interagency procedures and a common format for reporting incidents. The incident portal is hosted by FAA, but due to its security policy, other agencies are not able to access the

---

[35]For more information on Lightsquared, see National Space-Based Positioning, Navigation, and Timing Systems Engineering Forum, *Assessment of Lightsquared Terrestrial Broadband System Effects on GPS Receivers and GPS-dependent Applications* (June 2011).

[36]Signed by the Secretaries of Defense, Homeland Security, and Transportation in the spring of 2013, the 2012 *Federal Radionavigation Plan* reflects the official PNT policy and planning for the federal government.

portal.[37] Other activities remain incomplete, including those related to identifying GPS backup-system requirements and determining suitability of backup capabilities. DHS officials cited a variety of reasons why they have not made additional progress, such as insufficient staffing and budget constraints. With respect to insufficient staffing, DHS's PNT Program Management Office, which leads the agency's IDM efforts, has three full-time staff members, one of whom is currently working in another component of DHS. With respect to budget constraints, DHS officials in the PNT Program Management Office stated that it is difficult to obtain financial resources in the current constrained budget environment. While DHS is in the process of formally implementing and standardizing procedures for information sharing among agency PNT operations centers when GPS disruptions occur, it does not have plans intended to address some other IDM activities, such as those related to development of GPS backup requirements and analysis of alternatives for backup capabilities.

Additionally, stakeholders expressed concern that DHS's IDM efforts are separated from other critical infrastructure protection efforts within DHS, but DHS has indicated that a new interagency task force will increase coordination between these efforts. Specifically, DHS's National Protection and Programs Directorate (NPPD) leads and manages efforts to protect the nation's 16 critical infrastructure sectors, but the PNT Program Management Office, within the Office of the Chief Information Officer, leads DHS's IDM efforts, as shown in figure 3. Members of the Advisory Board and the GPS experts from academic and other research institutions we spoke with expressed concern that this organizational structure means that GPS management does not receive the same level of attention and resources as the agency's other efforts to protect key national assets. DHS previously acknowledged that the agency's GPS efforts were event-driven, that resources were provided on an ad-hoc basis, and that NPPD was uniquely structured to fulfill many of NSPD-39's objectives, given its role of developing risk-mitigation strategies for critical infrastructure protection efforts. However, regarding this organization, DHS officials said that GPS expertise has been within the Office of the Chief Information Officer since DHS's creation and that the positions were originally hired to fulfill other DHS missions. As PNT

---

[37]Specifically, the incident portal does not allow user access for anyone outside FAA's firewall Intranet domain. FAA and DHS officials are working on a variety of solutions and, according to DHS officials, expect to have the issue resolved in fiscal year 2014.

issues became more prevalent, these positions evolved into the PNT Program Management Office. The officials noted that through a new interagency task force formed in April 2013, NPPD will have increased involvement in the agency's IDM efforts.

Figure 3: Separation of GPS Program Management and Infrastructure Protection Management within DHS

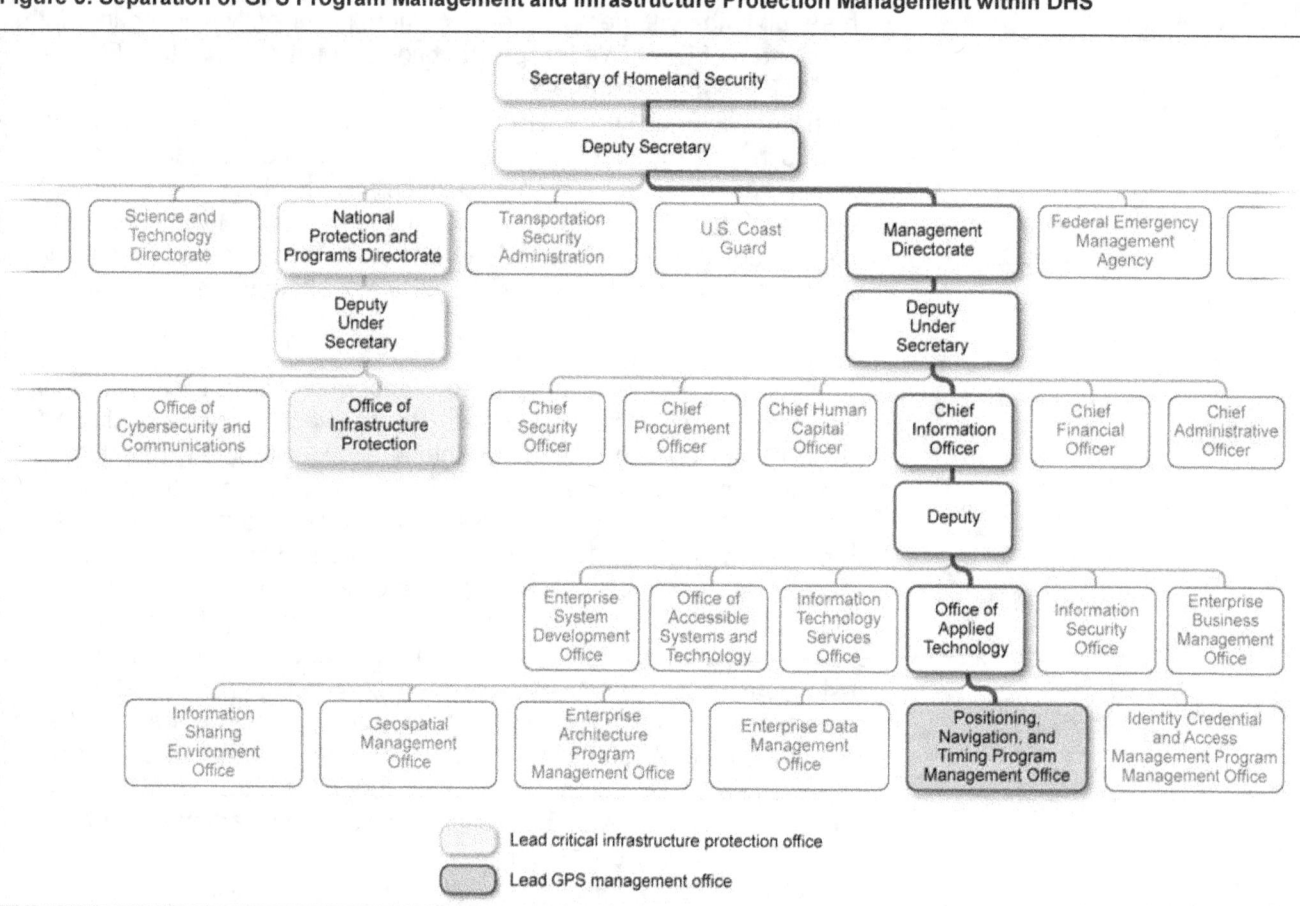

Source: GAO analysis of DHS information.

Figure 4 provides a timeline of DOT's and DHS's efforts to provide GPS backup capabilities since the issuance of NSPD-39 in 2004.

GAO-14-15 Impact of GPS Disruptions

Figure 4: Timeline of Key Events in DOT and DHS Efforts to Provide GPS Backup Capabilities, 2004-2012

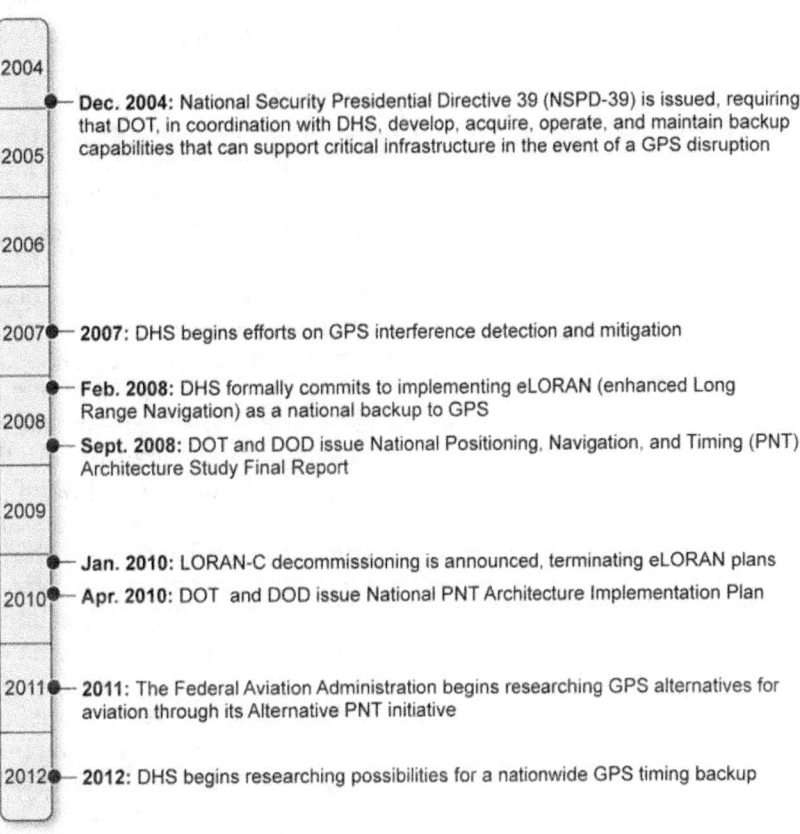

2004

Dec. 2004: National Security Presidential Directive 39 (NSPD-39) is issued, requiring that DOT, in coordination with DHS, develop, acquire, operate, and maintain backup capabilities that can support critical infrastructure in the event of a GPS disruption

2005

2006

2007 — **2007:** DHS begins efforts on GPS interference detection and mitigation

Feb. 2008: DHS formally commits to implementing eLORAN (enhanced Long Range Navigation) as a national backup to GPS

2008

Sept. 2008: DOT and DOD issue National Positioning, Navigation, and Timing (PNT) Architecture Study Final Report

2009

Jan. 2010: LORAN-C decommissioning is announced, terminating eLORAN plans

2010 — **Apr. 2010:** DOT and DOD issue National PNT Architecture Implementation Plan

2011 — **2011:** The Federal Aviation Administration begins researching GPS alternatives for aviation through its Alternative PNT initiative

2012 — **2012:** DHS begins researching possibilities for a nationwide GPS timing backup

Source: NSPD-39 and GAO analysis of DOT and DHS information.

DOT and DHS Efforts Have Been Hampered by a Lack of Effective Collaboration

In addition to the challenges described above, DOT and DHS's ability to provide for backup capabilities as specified in the presidential directive has been hampered by a lack of effective collaboration. In prior work, we have identified key elements of effective collaboration that can help enhance and sustain collaboration among federal agencies, thereby maximizing performance and results.[38] Specifically, we have previously found that key elements of effective collaboration include clearly defining

---

[38]GAO-12-1022; GAO-06-15.

(1) roles, responsibilities, and authorities; (2) outcomes and monitoring progress toward outcomes; and (3) written agreements regarding how agencies will collaborate. DOT and DHS have not followed these practices; for example:

- **Roles and responsibilities**. DOT and DHS have not clearly defined what each agency's respective roles, responsibilities, and authorities are in terms of satisfying the presidential directive to provide GPS backup capabilities. Defining roles and responsibilities ensures that agencies have clearly articulated and agreed on which entity will do what and what is expected of each party. Various discussions we had with DOT and DHS officials indicated there is considerable confusion and lack of clarity between the agencies about what their roles, responsibilities, and authorities are, despite the guidance in NSPD-39. For example, DOT officials told us that they handle backup capabilities for aviation, but they depend on DHS and industry to provide backup capabilities for the other critical infrastructure sectors. DOT officials questioned why DOT would provide backup capabilities for non-transportation sectors and whether doing so would make sense. The DOT officials highlighted that sectors look to DHS for cross-sector capabilities to protect key national assets, such as GPS, and that DHS is better positioned to lead this effort given its mission and experience with managing and mitigating risks to critical infrastructure sectors. However, DHS officials we contacted told us that NSPD-39 places lead responsibility with DOT, not DHS. They stated that DHS has no legal basis or other authority to require that GPS users take measures to mitigate GPS disruptions by having backup capabilities in place. DHS officials also said that it may be industries' and individual sectors' responsibilities to ensure their systems have GPS backup capabilities, in coordination with their SSA. A DOD official and the GPS experts from academic and other research institutions we contacted also noted that it is not clear what entity or agency oversees GPS risk management for the different sectors and whether DHS has authority to require sectors to demonstrate that they have backup capabilities.

Further, stakeholders highlighted that it is unclear how the NSPD-39 backup-capabilities requirement fits in with the NIPP risk management framework DHS uses for critical infrastructure protection. Specifically, DOT and DHS officials noted that NSPD-39 predates the issuance of the first NIPP in 2006, which, as previously described, established the critical infrastructure protection risk management framework. As such, DOT and DHS officials, a DOD official, members of the Advisory Board, and the GPS experts from academic and other research institutions we contacted said that the NSPD-39 backup-capabilities requirement may be outdated and could require updating to better reflect current risk management guidance that, DOT officials added, would include operational mitigations in addition to backup systems. For example, DHS officials noted that the NIPP risk management framework indicates that SSAs are responsible for working with DHS to coordinate infrastructure protection for their sector, including backup capabilities. One DHS official said that his goal would be to have each critical infrastructure sector's Sector-Specific Plan address GPS disruptions.[39]

- **Outcomes and monitoring progress**. DOT and DHS have not established clear, agreed-upon outcomes that clarify what would satisfy the NSPD-39 backup-capabilities requirement, and neither agency has been consistently monitoring its progress. Establishing clear outcomes for efforts that require collaboration ensures that agencies have agreed on how they will satisfy mutual responsibilities and what specifically they are working toward. DOT's and DHS's confusion about roles described above indicates that the agencies have not done so. Additional statements made by the agencies also indicate that there may still be uncertainty about the desired outcome. For example, while DHS officials said that it might be each individual sector's responsibility to provide its own GPS backup solutions, DOT officials stated that individual solutions for every sector would be redundant and inefficient and that DOT does not desire a sector-based architecture for GPS backup capabilities. Additionally, DHS officials told us that a single, domestic backup to GPS is not needed, and DOT officials told us that a single backup solution fulfilling all users' needs would not be practical. Nevertheless, DOT officials stated that the Coast Guard's decommissioning of LORAN-C was a loss for the robustness of GPS backup capabilities, especially given that both DOT and DHS had supported the upgrading of LORAN-C to eLORAN as a national GPS backup.

- **Written agreements regarding collaboration**. DOT and DHS have not documented their agreements regarding how they will collaborate to satisfy their NSPD-39 backup-capabilities requirement. In prior work, we have found that the action of two agencies articulating roles

---

[39]As required by the NIPP, each SSA develops a Sector-Specific Plan to detail risk management in its critical infrastructure sector.

and responsibilities and a common outcome into a written document is a powerful collaboration tool.[40] Accordingly, we have recommended many times that collaborations benefit from formal written agreements, such as a memorandum of understanding or agreement. While the agencies have individual mitigation efforts that contribute to fulfilling the NSPD-39 backup-capabilities requirement, as described above, they do not have a written agreement that considers all of these efforts and provides a unified, holistic strategy for how the agencies are addressing their shared responsibility. According to DOT and DHS officials, the agencies are in the process of finalizing a written agreement on interagency procedures for information sharing among agency PNT operations centers when GPS disruptions occur (to which DOD will also be a signatory), but are not developing any type of written agreement memorializing how they will collaborate to satisfy the NSPD-39 backup-capabilities requirement.

Without clearly defining both roles and desired outcomes for efforts that require collaboration, DOT and DHS cannot ensure that they will satisfy mutual responsibilities. DOT stated that the rationale behind developing a national PNT architecture was the absence of coordinated interagency efforts on PNT, which could lead to uncoordinated research efforts, lack of clear developmental paths, potentially wasteful procurements, and inefficient deployment of resources. Additionally, DHS has reported that the well-established presence of effective backup capabilities could discourage threats to GPS in the first place. In light of the recent issuance of PPD-21 in February 2013, DOT, DHS, DOD, and the National Aeronautics and Space Administration formed a Critical Infrastructure Security and Resiliency scoping group to address the needed resiliency of critical infrastructure relying on GPS, and subsequently, the National Space-Based PNT Executive Steering Group established an Interagency IDM/Alternative PNT task force in April 2013. According to DHS officials, the task force plans to review and update planned IDM activities, and as previously noted, through the task force, NPPD will have increased involvement in the agency's IDM efforts. Such activities could provide an opportunity for DOT and DHS to address their challenges and uncertainties and document their agreements. However, as of July 2013, there was still confusion between the agencies on these future activities. For example, DOT officials stated that according to their current understanding based on guidance from the NCO, the task force would

---

[40]GAO-12-1022.

mostly monitor activities while DHS highlighted a broader scope of activity for the task force, including elevating awareness of critical sectors' dependencies on GPS.

Select Critical Infrastructure Sectors Employ Various Mitigation Strategies, but DHS Has Not Measured the Effectiveness of These Efforts

Sector-Specific Strategies to Mitigate GPS Disruptions Vary

Agency officials and industry representatives from the four critical infrastructure sectors we contacted said their sectors would generally be able to withstand short-term GPS disruptions and provided examples of strategies to mitigate GPS disruptions for aspects of sector operations, as follows.

- **Communications**. The communications sector, which uses GPS to synchronize timing of communications and for location-based services, employs a range of strategies to mitigate GPS disruptions. For example, at large critical communication nodes (e.g., mobile wireless and wireline-switching centers, satellite control centers), atomic clocks are often deployed to backup GPS. However, some of the most precise timing mechanisms may not be deployed widely across communications networks, and the type and level of redundancies vary across the network and across industry providers. Communications sector industry representatives believe GPS disruptions lasting over 24 hours would likely cause interruption of mobile communication services because call handoffs between cell sites would begin to fail.

- **Energy**. For one aspect of the energy sector—the bulk power system—DOE officials and energy sector industry representatives told us that the sector uses GPS to get frequent time measurements on the state of the system, but that the industry does not rely on GPS to operate the system at this time.[41] The representatives noted that the bulk power system has built-in redundancies and, in the event of a GPS disruption, could rely on other systems that provide less frequent time measurements.

- **Financial services**. According to Department of the Treasury officials, the financial services sector primarily relies on atomic clocks to time-stamp financial transactions; GPS is used as a secondary timing source in the communications protocols of these transactions. In the event of a GPS disruption, Treasury officials noted that the financial services sector has a risk management process in place, which includes hardware, software, and operational procedures to detect and mitigate any disruptions in communications.

- **Transportation systems**. Within the transportation systems sector, for aviation, FAA officials said that multiple legacy navigation systems that are not reliant on GPS signals can enable aircraft to fly and land in the event of a GPS disruption.[42] DHS officials noted that alternate means of navigation, such as radar and visual references to landmarks, are available for maritime users. An industry representative and a TSA official from the rail and commercial vehicle segments of the transportation systems sector, respectively, said that they do not currently need extensive GPS mitigation efforts since other means, such as maps and cell phone communication, can be used for navigation.

According to critical infrastructure sector agency officials and industry representatives we contacted, three of the four sectors have initiated efforts to study GPS vulnerability and potential mitigations, but have not yet implemented sector-wide mitigation efforts for various reasons. Some stakeholders told us they focus mitigation efforts on higher-priority threats. For example, energy sector industry representatives and financial services sector agency officials said that they are less concerned about

---

[41]The bulk power system refers to the facilities and control systems necessary for operating the electric transmission network and certain generation facilities needed for reliability.

[42]According to FAA officials, these legacy systems include the Very High Frequency Omni-Directional Range system, Instrument Landing System, and Distance Measuring Equipment.

GPS disruptions than other threats, like cybersecurity. The 2012 and 2013 annual summit agendas of a financial industry group dedicated to industry collaboration on critical security threats addressed cybersecurity threats and excluded threats from GPS disruptions. Sectors may be reluctant to bear significant costs for mitigation efforts because GPS disruptions are often perceived as low risk since the number of reported incidents is relatively low. For example, in 2012, only 44 incidents were reported to the Coast Guard, which fields reports of GPS disruptions. However, it is unclear the extent to which incidents have been properly reported. According to Coast Guard officials, GPS users are frequently unaware that the Coast Guard serves as the civilian focal point for reporting GPS disruptions, and oftentimes users do not report incidents because they assume a software glitch is the source of the problem. Furthermore, incidents caused by jammers (i.e., personal privacy devices) are often perceived as low impact events, generally due to their localized impact and popular use to avoid tracking of individuals. High-impact events, such as extreme solar storms, spoofing, and high-power jammers—which can impact a larger geographic area, or can have larger consequences in terms of safety, loss of life, and economic loss—are perceived as low probability.

DHS Has Not Measured the Effectiveness of the Sectors' Efforts to Mitigate GPS Disruptions

Although the sectors have taken steps to prepare for GPS disruptions, DHS has not measured the effectiveness of sectors' mitigation efforts to ensure sector resiliency against GPS disruptions. DHS officials told us that during 2013, DHS has been focused on increasing awareness of GPS embeddedness and potential disruptions within three sectors—the communications, information technology, and transportation systems sectors.[43] According to DHS and NCO officials, no plan or timeline has been developed or approved for identifying and assessing measures of effectiveness. DHS officials indicated it is not necessary to measure effectiveness of individual programs and that the absence of resilience measures for an individual program does not mean that DHS is not measuring overall resilience at the sector level.[44] Furthermore, DHS officials stated that the absence of a single measure at the program level

---

[43]DHS initiated this effort as part of the Interagency IDM/Alternative PNT task force.

[44]DHS referred us to its unreleased 2011-2012 National Annual Report. According to DHS, however, the report aggregates all the sector data to assess progress at a national level, and does not specify individual sectors or their measurements.

GAO-14-15 Impact of GPS Disruptions

may be for several reasons, including that the cost of data collection and analysis would be too great. However, the NIPP cites the importance of measuring program effectiveness and the use of performance metrics to track the effectiveness of protection programs. Specifically, the NIPP requires DHS to work with SSAs and sector partners to measure the effectiveness of critical infrastructure protection programs by establishing performance metrics that enable DHS to objectively assess improvements, track progress, establish accountability, document actual performance, provide feedback mechanisms, and inform decision-making. [45] More recently, PPD-21 emphasizes efforts to strengthen and maintain resilient critical infrastructure and requires DHS to use a metrics and analysis process to measure the nation's ability to manage and reduce risks to critical infrastructure. Additionally, PPD-21 emphasizes addressing resiliency in an environment of critical infrastructure's interconnectedness and interdependencies. As previously discussed, GPS supports interconnected systems both within and across sectors and GPS disruptions represent potential risks to critical infrastructure.

With regard to measuring effectiveness, we have previously recommended that DHS develop performance measures to assess the extent to which sector partners are taking actions to resolve resiliency gaps identified during various vulnerability assessments.[46] We have also previously recommended that outcome-based measures would assist DHS in assessing effectiveness of sector protection efforts.[47] GPS experts we contacted from academic and other research institutions noted that focusing on measuring outcomes—and not just on testing the GPS devices—in critical systems and sectors is important because several factors can affect mitigation effectiveness in the event of a GPS disruption: the GPS devices, the systems and equipment dependent on those devices, and the personnel and operational procedures that rely on

---

[45]As stated in the NIPP, the use of performance metrics is a critical step in the NIPP risk management process to enable DHS and the SSAs to objectively and quantitatively assess improvements in critical infrastructure sector protection and resiliency at the sector and national levels.

[46]GAO, *Critical Infrastructure Protection: DHS Efforts to Assess and Promote Resiliency Are Evolving but Program Management Could Be Strengthened*, GAO-10-772 (Washington, D.C.: Sept. 23, 2010).

[47]GAO, *Communications Networks: Outcome-Based Measures Would Assist DHS in Assessing Effectiveness of Cybersecurity Efforts*, GAO-13-275 (Washington, D.C.: Apr. 3, 2013).

GPS. While DHS requested SSA input for the NRE and stated they held tabletop exercises with other government agencies to test agency coordination processes in the event of a GPS disruption incident, DHS has not measured the effectiveness of mitigation efforts in terms of sector resiliency to GPS disruptions in the sectors we reviewed. Furthermore, the four Sector-Specific Plans submitted to DHS that we reviewed did not include any reference to GPS mitigation efforts. As a result of not having measurements, or a plan to assess the impact of GPS disruptions on critical infrastructure sectors, DHS cannot provide assurance that the critical infrastructure sectors would be able to maintain operations in the event of a GPS disruption without significant economic loss, or loss of life.

Measuring effectiveness of mitigation efforts on potential GPS disruptions as part of measuring sector resiliency is important because agency officials, industry representatives, and GPS experts have raised a number of concerns about the sectors' ability to sustain operations during GPS disruptions. For example, they raised the following concerns:

- **Low awareness**. Sector awareness of the extent to which GPS is embedded in their systems is frequently unknown and understated, thereby affecting their ability to plan appropriate mitigations. For example, DHS officials and the GPS experts from academic and other research institutions we contacted cited a GPS incident in San Diego that impaired normal operations in the communications, maritime, and aviation sectors, even though it was a short-term disruption, which according to communications sector industry representatives, should not have impaired operations because of the sector's backup and mitigation measures. Separately, in the maritime industry, we heard from Coast Guard officials that multiple shipboard systems are dependent on GPS and mariners may not be aware of the dependencies. In a United Kingdom maritime GPS disruption test, numerous alarms sounded on the ship's bridge due to the failure of different systems, and the test raised concerns that GPS signal loss could lead to hazardous conditions for mariners.

- **Sustainability**. The degree to which backup systems can sustain current levels of operations and users are able to operate legacy backup systems is unknown. Coast Guard officials indicated that mariners who are accustomed to relying on GPS may no longer have the skills or staff to adequately use legacy backup systems, and that the legacy systems may be less efficient, causing economic losses. For example, according to Coast Guard officials, if GPS were disrupted for a day or more in a major port, it could result in millions of dollars of losses due to inefficiencies in managing ship and cargo traffic.

- **Increasing dependency**. Use of GPS is growing and it is unclear what mitigations would be effective with increased GPS use. For example, in the energy sector, as GPS is increasingly used to monitor the bulk power system, reliance on GPS in the long term may become more critical in grid operations. According to a DOE official, DOE validated the lab tests of an academic expert who demonstrated the vulnerability of GPS-based bulk power system monitoring equipment to a spoofing attack and has efforts under way to determine the long-term implications of increasing GPS dependency. The aviation segment of the transportation systems sector will also be more dependent on GPS. As previously described, GPS will be the primary navigation aid under NextGen and FAA plans to eventually decommission much of the current legacy navigation systems and replace them with potentially new, alternative PNT systems currently being researched.[48] In the rail segment of the transportation systems sector, the use of GPS to provide safety benefits through positive train control is increasing, and DOT has indicated that degradation or loss of GPS could, in the future, result in rail network congestion or gridlock.

- **Sector interdependencies**. Interdependencies among sectors may not be well understood. For example, FAA reported that while its air traffic control systems have backup systems for GPS, its communication systems rely on the communications sector, which might experience some problems in the event of GPS disruptions. Therefore, one sector's lack of appropriate mitigation may affect other sectors.

- **Likelihood of disruptions**. According to the stakeholders, the likelihood of GPS disruptions could be growing and may be underestimated by sectors and DHS. DHS officials and the GPS experts from academic and other research institutions we contacted cited that an Internet search for "GPS jammer" yielded approximately 500,000 results. They noted that over time, as the technology advances, these jammers are likely to become smaller, more powerful, and less expensive, increasing the likelihood of disruptions.

---

[48]FAA is considering maintaining and modifying several legacy systems.

Additionally, in the last few years, a growing number of papers and industry presentations are available on the Internet that discuss or show the ability to spoof GPS receivers in multiple sectors, which agency officials said could increase the likelihood of spoofing. Furthermore, GPS experts indicated that the unintended interference produced by the introduction of new communication services near the GPS frequencies has the potential to greatly disrupt reception of the relatively weak GPS signal, and indicated the difficulty of estimating these disruptions in advance and isolating them.

Conclusions

GPS is essential to U.S. national security and is a key component in economic growth, safety, and national critical infrastructure sectors. As GPS becomes increasingly integrated into sectors' operations, it has become an invisible utility that users do not realize underpins their applications, leaving sectors potentially vulnerable to GPS disruptions. We recognize that risk assessments, such as the NRE, involve complex analysis and that conducting a risk assessment across multiple sectors of systems with many unknowns and little data is particularly challenging. Although DHS attempted to overcome these challenges, the NRE also lacks some of the key characteristics of risk assessments outlined in the NIPP and, as a result, is incomplete. As such, the NRE is limited in its usefulness to inform mitigation planning, priorities, and resource allocation. Furthermore, the lack of an overall DHS plan designed to address the NRE's shortcomings, such as lack of data, and enhance its risk assessment approach, such as by using available threat assessments, could hinder future public and private risk management of GPS. A plan and a time frame for developing a more complete data-driven risk assessment that also addresses the deficiencies in the NRE's assessment methodology would help DHS capitalize on progress it has made in conducting risk assessments and contribute to the more effective management of the increasing risks to the nation's critical infrastructure. Such steps also would provide DHS planners and other decision makers with insights into DHS's overall progress and a basis for determining what, if any, additional actions need to be taken.

Federal agencies and experts have reported that the inability to mitigate GPS disruptions could result in billions of dollars of economic loss. Critical infrastructure sectors have employed various strategies to mitigate GPS disruptions, but both the NRE and stakeholders we interviewed raised concerns that since sector risks are underestimated, growing, and interdependent, it is unclear whether such efforts are sufficient. Federal risk management policy requires DHS to work with SSAs and sector partners to measure the nation's ability to manage and reduce risks to critical infrastructure by using a metrics and analysis process. However, we found DHS has not measured the effectiveness of sector mitigation efforts to GPS disruptions. As a result, DHS cannot ensure that critical infrastructure sectors could sustain essential operations during GPS disruptions. The lack of agreed-upon metrics to measure the actual effectiveness of sector mitigation efforts hinders DHS's ability to objectively assess improvements, track progress, establish accountability, provide feedback mechanisms, or inform decision makers about the appropriateness of—or need for additional—mitigation activities. We previously recommended that DHS develop performance measures to assess the extent to which sector partners are taking actions to resolve resiliency gaps identified during the various vulnerability assessments. Measuring effectiveness of mitigation efforts on potential GPS disruptions as part of measuring sector resiliency is important because agency officials, industry representatives, and GPS experts have raised a number of concerns about the sectors' ability to sustain operations during GPS disruptions.

Although the President directed DOT, in coordination with DHS, to develop backup capabilities to mitigate GPS disruptions, the agencies have made limited progress amid continued uncertainty. Both agencies cited resource constraints—such as budget and staffing—as a reason why they have not made additional progress. Nevertheless, DOT and DHS have not defined their respective roles, responsibilities, and authorities or what agreed-upon outcome would satisfy the presidential directive. As a result, DOT and DHS cannot ensure that they will satisfy mutual responsibilities. Clearly delineating roles and responsibilities and agreed-upon outcomes and documenting these agreements would allow the agencies to address many of the uncertainties regarding fulfillment of their NSPD-39 backup-capabilities requirement, such as which agency is responsible for various key tasks, what role SSAs and industry should have, how NSPD-39 fits into the NIPP risk management framework, whether NSPD-39 is outdated, and others.

Recommendations for Executive Action

To ensure that the increasing risks of GPS disruptions to the nation's critical infrastructure are effectively managed, we recommend that the Secretary of Homeland Security take the following two actions:

- Increase the reliability and usefulness of the GPS risk assessment by developing a plan and time frame to collect relevant threat, vulnerability, and consequence data for the various critical infrastructure sectors, and periodically review the readiness of data to conduct a more data-driven risk assessment while ensuring that DHS's assessment approach is more consistent with the NIPP.

- As part of current critical infrastructure protection planning with SSAs and sector partners, develop and issue a plan and metrics to measure the effectiveness of GPS risk mitigation efforts on critical infrastructure resiliency.

To improve collaboration and address uncertainties in fulfilling the NSPD-39 backup-capabilities requirement, we recommend that the Secretaries of Transportation and Homeland Security take the following action:

- Establish a formal, written agreement that details how the agencies plan to address their shared responsibility. This agreement should address uncertainties, including clarifying and defining DOT's and DHS's respective roles, responsibilities, and authorities; establishing clear, agreed-upon outcomes; establishing how the agencies will monitor and report on progress toward those outcomes; and setting forth the agencies' plans for examining relevant issues, such as the roles of SSAs and industry, how NSPD-39 fits into the NIPP risk management framework, whether an update to the NSPD-39 is needed, or other issues as deemed necessary by the agencies.

Agency Comments and Our Evaluation

We provided a draft of this report to the Departments of Homeland Security, Transportation, and Commerce for their review and comment. DHS provided written comments (reprinted in app. II) and technical comments, which we incorporated as appropriate. DOT provided informal comments summarized below, and technical comments, which we incorporated as appropriate. Commerce had no comments.

In written comments, DHS concurred with two of our recommendations and noted activities that it will undertake to address those recommendations. In particular, DHS concurred with our recommendation to develop and issue a plan and metrics to measure the effectiveness of GPS risk mitigation efforts, and our recommendation that DHS and DOT establish a formal written agreement that details how the agencies plan to address their shared responsibility.

However, DHS did not concur with our recommendation related to increasing the reliability and usefulness of the GPS risk assessment and expressed concern about our evaluation of the NRE. DHS stated that it did not agree with this recommendation because DHS officials and subject matter experts believe the existing NRE analysis has sufficiently characterized the risk environment, and that our characterization of the NRE's incorporation of best practices is inaccurate. Specifically, DHS disagreed with our analysis about the extent to which the NRE met NIPP criteria that risk assessments be complete, reproducible, defensible, and documented and provided reasons for its disagreement. For example, regarding our analysis of the NRE's incompleteness, DHS stated that the NIPP does not require that a risk assessment consider all, or even a minimum number of, critical infrastructure sectors to be complete. Rather, DHS noted, the NIPP states that the risk assessment methodology must assess consequence, vulnerability, and threat for every defined risk scenario. Regarding our analysis that the NRE was not being widely used, DHS noted that we do not reference a second, concurrent report directed at mitigation of GPS risks. DHS stated that the NRE was, by design, meant to primarily support the National Executive Committee for Space-Based PNT's high-level, interagency policy role, and that the committee and its staff had provided positive feedback. Based on its reasons for non-concurrence, DHS requested that we consider this recommendation resolved and closed.

We disagree with DHS's assertion that our characterization of the NRE is inaccurate. We have added additional text to clarify that based on the NIPP criteria we determined, overall, that the NRE was incomplete because each aspect of the NRE's risk assessment—threat, vulnerability, and consequence—was incomplete. Regarding our analysis that the NRE was not reproducible, we found that the NRE does not conform to the NIPP because it is based entirely on subjective judgments of panelists. If different panelists were chosen, the results might have been different. Subject matter experts we interviewed told us they were skeptical about the quality of the panel deliberations, and characterized the members' judgments as "educated guesses." Regarding if the results were defensible, we continue to believe that potentially useful statistical techniques are only as valid as the underlying data, and that a core problem of the NRE methodology was that it did not document how the panel experts were chosen; the opinions of those experts were the basis for virtually all the data in the NRE. For example, at a minimum the quality of DHS's panel selection would have been more transparent to the independent reviewer (as well as the participants) if DHS detailed exactly what sector and GPS expertise were required for each panel and how well the participating panelists covered these areas of expertise. After DHS officials told us that they had little documentary support for the NRE, we narrowed our request and asked DHS officials to defend and provide support for some of their key conclusions, but they did not provide it.

Several industry and federal representatives we interviewed questioned whether the panels had sufficiently broad expertise to capture the full scope of GPS vulnerabilities within sectors. Regarding documentation, as we reported, the NRE did include some elements of documentation that were consistent with the NIPP. However, DHS stated that with limited data, its methodology depended on the expert judgment of the NRE panels. Thus, as previously noted, documenting the rigor of the panel selection process was crucial to the validity of the NRE. Nevertheless, DHS did not provide documentation, either in the NRE or in subsequent information requests, on how the subject matter experts were selected. This and other documentation issues, such as not fully reporting the underlying data supporting the risk calculations, also affect the NRE's reproducibility and defensibility.

Regarding our point that the NRE has not been widely used to inform risk mitigation priorities, DHS commented that we fail to mention that the National Executive Committee also requested a mitigation assessment. The mitigation study was discussed in our risk mitigation section of the report, and we have included additional information on the study. However, since the studies were done concurrently, the mitigation study was not informed by the NRE. Among other things, the report identifies best practices to mitigate risk to GPS receivers rather than using the NRE to develop a mitigation plan to reduce the risks the NRE identified and guide resource allocation, as required by the NIPP. Regarding the intended use of the NRE, the NCO told us that the study was intended to help inform senior government officials about risk associated with GPS use, not just the National Executive Committee or NCO. We have added language to clarify that NCO officials stated that they and the National Executive Committee were generally satisfied with the NRE. However, as we noted in the report, the NRE was distributed to other agencies and TSA officials told us that they are not using the NRE and did not see the relevance to TSA, and officials from the Departments of Defense and Energy told us that the NRE was not helpful in managing GPS risks.

DHS commented that data on GPS risk factors have not improved and in its technical comments DHS noted that it has commissioned a study to obtain better data. However, while we recognize that obtaining better data is a challenge, we continue to believe that DHS should increase the reliability and usefulness of the GPS risk assessment by developing a plan and time frame to collect relevant threat, vulnerability, and consequence data for the various critical infrastructure sectors, and periodically review the readiness of data to conduct a more data-driven risk assessment while ensuring that DHS's assessment approach is more consistent with the NIPP. For example, DHS could use the classified threat assessment that was completed too late to be included in the NRE, and it could proactively acquire and use private sector threat assessments. We believe such actions will help DHS develop a more rigorous, reliable assessment to inform risk mitigation planning and resource allocation. Consistent with our recommendation, DHS has initiated an effort to survey and better understand the vulnerabilities of critical infrastructure sectors. In May 2013, DHS awarded funding to four companies to conduct a detailed survey report of existing civilian GPS receiver use within two critical infrastructure sectors, among other things. A later phase of this effort, according to DHS documentation, is to explore other sectors. This is a good first step toward gathering the kind of information DHS needs to conduct more data-driven risk assessments in the future. The National Executive Committee's 5-year plan recommends that DHS institute a risk management approach to assess threats, vulnerabilities, and potential consequences to interference to GPS signals and examine the best opportunities to mitigate those risks. Because of the shortcomings we found in the NRE, we do not believe that DHS has instituted an adequate risk management approach to address the risks associated with GPS interference. Although DHS requested that we consider this recommendation resolved and closed, we disagree and believe that our recommendation is still needed to ensure that DHS develops a plan to gather the data required for risk assessment and risk management.

In providing comments on the draft report, DOT declined to take a position on the recommendations but agreed to consider our recommendation to improve collaboration and address uncertainties in fulfilling the NSPD-39 backup-capabilities requirement. DOT stated that the agency has worked closely with DHS on PNT-related activities but it welcomed the opportunity to have agency roles clarified in a formal, written agreement. DOT also reiterated that the agency's views are consistent with the National PNT Architecture report's "greater common denominator" strategy described in this report. DOT noted that GPS dependency and the ability to handle a GPS disruption are not well understood and will not be well understood until there is a "real-world" incident or test scenario to evaluate. DOT also noted that the recently formed Interagency IDM/Alternative PNT task force needs to expand its scope beyond monitoring activities.

We are sending copies of this report to the Secretary of Homeland Security, the Secretary of Transportation, the Secretary of Commerce and interested congressional committees. In addition, the report is available at no charge on our website at http://www.gao.gov.

If you or your staff have any questions concerning this report, please contact Mark Goldstein at (202) 512-2834 or goldsteinm@gao.gov, or Joseph Kirschbaum at (202) 512-9971 or kirschbaumj@gao.gov. Contact points for our Offices of Congressional Relations and Public Affairs may be found on the last page of this report. Key contributors to this report are listed in appendix III.

Mark Goldstein
Director, Physical Infrastructure Issues

Joseph Kirschbaum
Acting Director, Homeland Security and Justice Issues

Appendix I: Objectives, Scope, and Methodology

We reviewed (1) the extent to which the Department of Homeland Security (DHS) has assessed the risks of Global Positioning System (GPS) disruptions and their potential effects on the nation's critical infrastructure, (2) the extent to which the Department of Transportation (DOT) and DHS have planned or developed backup capabilities or other strategies to mitigate the effects of GPS disruptions, and (3) what strategies, if any, selected critical infrastructure sectors employ to mitigate the effects of GPS disruptions, and any remaining challenges they face. We focused on civilian uses of GPS and on the following four critical infrastructure sectors: communications, energy, financial services, and transportation systems. We focused on civilian, as opposed to military, uses of GPS because the majority of GPS applications and users are civilian. We selected these sectors because of their dependence on GPS, interdependence with other sectors, inclusion in DHS's GPS National Risk Estimate (NRE), and designation as critical sectors.

To address these issues, we interviewed or obtained written comments from federal and state government officials, industry representatives, and GPS subject matter experts. Specifically, we contacted government officials from agencies involved in GPS governance, such as the Department of Defense (DOD), DOT, and DHS. To obtain views from state government officials, we contacted members of the U.S. States & Local Government Subcommittee of the Civil GPS Service Interface Committee, which is a forum established by DOT to exchange information about GPS with the civilian user community. In selecting these members, we asked the chair of the Subcommittee to identify a list of potential state government officials, and we ensured the officials represented a variety of states, geographical locations, and GPS uses. We also contacted the Sector-Specific Agency (SSA) for each of the sectors we studied, as follows: DHS's Office of Cybersecurity and Communications (CS&C) for the communications sector, the Department of Energy (DOE) for the energy sector, the Department of the Treasury for the financial services sector, and DOT, the Transportation Security Administration (TSA), and the U.S. Coast Guard for the transportation systems sector. To obtain views from industry representatives, we contacted the Sector Coordinating Council (SCC) for each of the sectors we studied and selected industry participants to interview based on input from a

designated spokesperson for each SCC.[1] For the energy and
transportation systems sectors, we contacted each sub-sector, although
not all sub-sectors participated or provided us with written responses, as
shown in table 1.[2] Industry representatives from the financial services
sector declined to respond to our requests for information. Additionally,
we contacted various GPS subject matter experts, including members of
the National Space-Based Positioning, Navigation, and Timing (PNT)
Advisory Board (Advisory Board), which is a federal advisory committee
that provides independent advice to the U.S. government on GPS
matters. We requested that our Advisory Board liaison invite all members
to participate, and members participated based on their availability. Views
expressed by members of the Advisory Board do not necessarily
represent the official position of the Board as a whole. We also attended a
formal meeting of the Advisory Board in May 2013. In selecting experts to
contact, we considered relevant published literature; their experience as
reflected in publications, testimonies, positions held, and their
biographies; recommendations from the Institute of Navigation (a non-
profit professional society dedicated to PNT); and other stakeholders'
recommendations. See table 1 for a list of the stakeholders we contacted.

---

[1]SCCs serve as the principal entity for coordinating with the federal government on critical
infrastructure protection activities and issues. SCCs are self-organized, self-run, and self-
governed bodies composed of critical infrastructure owners and operators.

[2]The energy sector is comprised of the electricity sub-sector and the oil and natural gas
sub-sector. The transportation systems sector is comprised of six modal sub-sectors:
aviation, highway and motor carrier, maritime, mass transit, pipelines, and railroad. As of
July 2013, the maritime sub-sector does not have an SCC.

Table 1: Government Officials, Industry Representatives, and Subject Matter Experts We Contacted

Stakeholder groups	Stakeholder
Federal government agency officials	Department of Commerce: • National Oceanic and Atmospheric Administration (NOAA) – including the National Environmental Satellite, Data, and Information Service; National Ocean Service; National Weather Service; and the Office of Oceanic and Atmospheric Research
	DOD: • Office of the Secretary of Defense • U.S. Air Force
	DOE: • Office of Electricity Delivery and Energy Reliability
	DHS: • Coast Guard – including the Navigation Center (NAVCEN) • Federal Emergency Management Agency • National Protection and Programs Directorate (NPPD) – including CS&C and the Office of Infrastructure Protection • Office of the Chief Information Officer • Science and Technology Directorate • TSA
	DOT: • Federal Aviation Administration (FAA) • Federal Highway Administration • Maritime Administration • Office of the Secretary of Transportation • Research and Innovative Technology Administration
	Department of the Treasury • Office of Domestic Finance
	National Coordination Office for Space-Based PNT (NCO)
State government officials[a]	Alaska
	Maryland
	Oregon
	Texas
	Washington
	Association of Public-Safety Communications Officials

Stakeholder groups	Stakeholder
Industry representatives	Communications SCC: • Alliance for Telecommunications Industry Solutions • AT&T • CenturyLink • CTIA–The Wireless Association • Motorola • National Cable and Telecommunications Association • Sprint • USTelecom
	Energy SCC: • Electricity Sub-Sector: North American Electric Reliability Corporation
	Transportation Systems SCC: • Aviation Modal Sub-Sector: Airports Council International • Highway and Motor Carrier Modal Sub-Sector: Owner-Operator Independent Drivers Association • Pipeline Modal Sub-Sector: Chevron
	GPS device manufacturer: • Garmin International
GPS subject matter experts	Advisory Board members: • Per Enge, Stanford University • Martin Faga, MITRE • James Geringer, Environmental Systems Research Institute • Kirk Lewis, GPS Independent Review Team[b] • James McCarthy, U.S. Air Force Academy • Ruth Nellan, Jet Propulsion Laboratory • Bradford Parkinson, Stanford University
	Experts from academic and other research institutions: • Jim Doherty, Institute of Navigation • Chris Hegarty, MITRE • Todd Humphreys, University of Texas at Austin

Source: GAO.

[a]States were contacted through the U.S. States & Local Government Subcommittee of the Civil GPS Service Interface Committee.

[b]This participant is not an official member of the Advisory Board, but serves as an expert/advisor to the Chair of the Advisory Board.

To review the extent to which DHS has assessed the risks of GPS disruptions and their potential effects on the nation's critical infrastructure, we compared DHS's efforts to established risk assessment criteria and contacted GPS stakeholders. Specifically, as the centerpiece of DHS's GPS risk assessment efforts, we reviewed DHS's 2012 GPS NRE and compared it to the risk assessment criteria established in the National

Infrastructure Protection Plan (NIPP), originally issued by DHS in 2006 and updated in 2009.[3] To learn more about the NRE's scope, methodology, and conduct, we interviewed the DHS officials responsible for authoring the NRE and reviewed related documentation. We also reviewed the DHS commissioned study that was requested in conjunction with the NRE. Additionally, we reviewed other assessments that consider GPS risks—including threat, vulnerability, and consequence—from DHS and others. For example, documentation we reviewed included DOT's 2001 Vulnerability Assessment of the Transportation Infrastructure Relying on the GPS, the Homeland Security Institute's 2005 GPS Vulnerability Assessment, MITRE's 2010 Coast Guard C4IT GPS Vulnerabilities Assessment, and the North American Electric Reliability Corporation's 2012 Extended Loss of GPS Impact on Reliability whitepaper, among others. Additionally, we interviewed or obtained written responses from the government officials, industry representatives, and GPS subject matter experts identified in table 2 to obtain their views on the NRE and to assess whether the NRE is being used to inform sector risk management efforts.

To review the extent to which DOT and DHS have planned or developed backup capabilities or other strategies to mitigate the effects of GPS disruptions, we contacted GPS stakeholders, examined agency documentation, and reviewed relevant federal policies and directives. Specifically, we interviewed DOT and DHS officials as identified in table 2. We also reviewed documentation from these agencies on the efforts they have undertaken. For example, DHS documentation we reviewed included materials related to IDM efforts and the draft 2013 Interagency Memorandum of Agreement with Respect to Support to Users of the Navstar GPS, among others. DOT documentation we reviewed included the 2006 National PNT Architecture Terms of Reference, the 2010 National PNT Architecture Implementation Plan and the 2008 DOD National PNT Architecture Study Final Report, the 2008 Memorandum of Agreement between DOD and DOT on Civil Use of the GPS, and documentation related to FAA's Alternative PNT initiative, among others. We also reviewed other key documentation related to GPS, such as the 2012 Federal Radionavigation Plan. We compared this information to NSPD-39 and also reviewed other relevant policies, such as the President's 2010 National Space Policy of the U.S.A. We also interviewed

---

[3]We have applied the NIPP criteria to risk assessments in numerous reports.

or obtained written responses from the government officials, industry representatives, and GPS subject matter experts identified in table 2 to obtain their views on DOT and DHS's efforts or for context sophistication. For example, we interviewed the NCO and reviewed meeting minutes from the National Executive Committee for Space-Based PNT and its Executive Steering Group and reviewed its *National Five-Year Plan for Space-Based PNT for Fiscal Years 2009-2013*. Additionally, we compared DOT and DHS's efforts against our criteria on key elements of effective collaboration.[4]

To review what strategies, if any, selected critical infrastructure sectors employ to mitigate the effects of GPS disruption, and any remaining challenges they face, we contacted GPS stakeholders identified in table 2 and reviewed relevant reports and whitepapers from these entities. We also interviewed the SSAs for each sector, as described above and identified in table 2, and reviewed the Sector-Specific Plans for each sector to assess if GPS is addressed. We reviewed the NIPP risk management framework for guidance on measuring the effectiveness of sector risk mitigation efforts. Additionally, we reviewed literature and presentations from academia, the Space Weather Prediction Center within NOAA's National Weather Service, and other government agencies, GPS subject matter experts and research institutions. We received Coast Guard data on the number of GPS incidents reported to NAVCEN. We did not assess the reliability of these data because they did not materially affect our findings, conclusions, or recommendations. We also interviewed or obtained written responses from the government officials, industry representatives, and GPS subject matter experts identified in table 2 to obtain their views on sector mitigation efforts and factors that affect sector mitigation efforts.

We conducted this review from November 2012 to November 2013 in accordance with generally accepted government auditing standards. Those standards require that we plan and perform the audit to obtain sufficient and appropriate evidence to provide a reasonable basis for our findings and conclusions based on our audit objectives. We believe that the evidence obtained provides a reasonable basis for our findings and conclusions based on our audit objectives.

---

[4]GAO-12-1022; GAO-06-15.

Appendix II: Comments from the Department of Homeland Security

U.S. Department of Homeland Security
Washington, DC 20528

**Homeland
Security**

September 27, 2013

Mark Goldstein
Director, Physical Infrastructure Issues
U.S. Government Accountability Office
441 G Street, NW
Washington, DC 20548

Joseph Kirschbaum
Acting Director, Homeland Security and Justice
U.S. Government Accountability Office
441 G Street, NW
Washington, DC 20548

Re: Draft Report GAO-14-15, "GPS DISRUPTIONS: Efforts to Assess Risks to Critical
       Infrastructure and Coordinate Agency Actions Should be Enhanced "

Dear Sirs:

Thank you for the opportunity to review and comment on this draft report. The U.S. Department
of Homeland Security (DHS) appreciates the U.S. Government Accountability Office's (GAO's)
work in planning and conducting its review and issuing this report.

DHS generally agrees with GAO's recommendations regarding engagement with Sector-Specific
Agencies (SSAs) on Global Positioning System (GPS) risk mitigation and the need to strengthen
coordination with interagency partners. However, program officials and subject matter experts
(SMEs) within DHS's National Protection and Program Directorate (NPPD), Office of
Infrastructure Protection (IP), and elsewhere are concerned about GAO's evaluation of the "DHS
National Risk Estimate: Risks to U.S. Critical Infrastructure from Global Positioning System
Disruptions" (NRE).

For example, the draft report states that the NRE has not been widely used to inform risk
mitigation priorities. Yet, the report does not mention that the National Executive Committee for
Space-Based Positioning, Navigation, and Timing (EXCOM) requested two assessments—one
on risk and one on mitigation—and tasked DHS as the lead for both assessments. This fact was
discussed with the GAO team and relevant supporting documentation provided during the audit.
It is important to note that the NRE was designed to address the risk assessment and purposefully
avoided substantial discussion of mitigation because the separate mitigation assessment effort
addressed this issue, including, but not limited to, best practices to mitigate GPS risks; GPS
industry products, initiatives, and market trends; summaries of current laws and regulations; and

GAO-14-15 Impact of GPS Disruptions

potential legislative, regulatory, and policy changes. The draft report also states that "the NRE
has not been widely used to inform risk mitigation priorities," which neither acknowledges nor
distinguishes the separate purposes of the two distinct reports that DHS developed in response to
EXCOM's request.

In addition, the primary customer for the NRE was EXCOM, which requested that DHS
complete a civil GPS risk and mitigation assessment. The draft report states GAO "found the
NRE has not been widely used," yet the NRE was, by design, meant to primarily support
EXCOM's high-level, interagency policy role. Along these lines, both EXCOM and its staff at
the National Coordinating Office for Position, Navigation, and Timing have provided positive
feedback on the NRE, which was also not fully documented in the draft report.

The draft report also indicates that the NRE was incomplete and does not fully conform to the
National Infrastructure Protection Plan (NIPP) because it considered just four critical
infrastructure sectors. However, NIPP criteria do not require that a risk assessment consider
all—or even a minimum number of—critical infrastructure sectors to be complete. Rather, the
NIPP states that "the [risk assessment] methodology must assess consequence, vulnerability, and
threat for every defined risk scenario and follow the more specific guidance for each of these."
For each scenario, DHS assessed—using the best available information—both the likelihood
(threat and vulnerability) and impact (consequence). While developing the NRE, DHS
recognized that there were limitations in data availability with regard to some risk factors and
documented these limitations in the NRE. For example, the NRE included overviews of data
sources in Chapters 3 and 4 and noted challenges stemming from uncertainty and the absence of
data in Chapter 4 and Annex F, where the NRE states, "SMEs noted that the absence of accurate
data about incidents of GPS disruptions made it challenging to estimate the likelihood of
scenarios." The NIPP also recognized such challenges and encouraged conducting estimates on
specific criteria—e.g., the psychological impacts or the number of fatalities, injuries, and
illnesses stemming from a specific scenario—when "feasible."

In addition, the draft report states that "the NRE does not conform to the NIPP because it is not
reproducible," and that others cannot reasonably review and reproduce the NRE's efforts
because decisions on expert selection were not documented in the NRE. Risk analysis best
practices generally require that the methodology used have a reproducible approach to analyzing
and developing findings from the information gleaned from such SMEs. Annexes C ("NRE Risk
Assessment and Monte Carlo Simulation Methodology") and F ("Likelihood Workshop
Findings") of the NRE clearly outline the process used to capture data (i.e., frequency estimates
for specific scenarios) from SMEs, as well as the approach to integrate the various estimates.
The NRE also captured the uncertainty of SME judgments (e.g., in Annexes E ("Consequence
Workshop Findings") and G ("Sector Alternative Futures Workshop Findings")) and conducted a
Monte Carlo simulation[1] to demonstrate ranges for NPPD findings. This approach prevented

---

[1] Monte Carlo simulation is a computerized mathematical technique that allows people to account for risk in
quantitative analysis and decision making. Monte Carlo simulation uses a random sampling of data to calculate
results based on a probability distribution. It is often used to simulate mathematical models and is ideal for models
with small sample sizes. For this reason, a Monte Carlo simulation was chosen to further analyze the risk results for
the NRE.

2

reporting false precision so that findings originating with different SMEs would fall within the range of uncertainty already identified.

DHS agrees that, if the scope of the NRE had been expanded to address additional aspects of GPS risk or additional sectors and sub-sectors, it would have allowed for fuller discussions and broader perspectives. Nevertheless, what is most important to any evaluation of the NRE being reproducible is the question of whether another entity using the same raw data that DHS collected could follow the same procedures and develop reproducible results. DHS program officials and SMEs believe the answer to this question is yes and the NRE's more focused assessment approach, as conducted and within the scope defined by the NRE, is reproducible.

The importance of how DHS processed raw data collected from SMEs is noted in how GAO addressed the extent to which it found the NRE "defensible." The draft report states, "NRE's calculations of risk are not sufficiently transparent to assess whether the risk estimates are defensible and free of significant error." DHS disagrees with this conclusion, which may stem from a misreading of the NIPP criteria and limited review of the NRE's underlying data and analysis. Although DHS did not include all the raw data as lengthy spreadsheets within an NRE annex, the data, including the results of the Monte Carlo simulations, are made available to researchers who may wish to review it. It is important to note that during this audit, GAO did not request, nor receive, all the raw data; however, DHS provided detailed, technical answers to GAO's general questions. NPPD IP program officials and SMEs do not believe that GAO's review of these answers alone provides a sufficient basis to make judgments about the defensibility of the underlying data and analysis.

Lastly, it appears that GAO may have misunderstood the NIPP criteria for well-documented risk assessment may have been misunderstood. This criteria requires that a "methodology and the assessment must clearly document what information is used and how it is synthesized to generate a risk estimate. Any assumptions, weighting factors, and subjective judgments need to be transparent to the user of the methodology, its audience, and others who are expected to use the results." Each of these factors was documented in NRE chapters (covering its *Scope* and *Analytic Assumptions*), along with Annexes C, E, F, and G. The Annexes detail how the data were collected, where subjective judgments were used, and how the data were synthesized. The draft report states that "the NRE does not conform to the NIPP's principles "because ... it does not document how the subject matter experts ... were selected." To the contrary, the NIPP does not require a detailed explanation of how each SME was chosen. The NRE does provide a list of every SME used (Annex I) and explains that the SMEs were either recommended by the SSA, another sector, or GPS SME.

The draft report contained three recommendations, two with which the Department concurs and one with which it non-concurs. Specifically, GAO recommended the Secretary of Homeland Security:

Recommendation 1: Increase the reliability and usefulness of the GPS risk assessment by developing a plan and timeframe to collect relevant threat, vulnerability, and consequence data for the various critical infrastructure sectors, and periodically review the readiness of data to

3

conduct a more data-driven risk assessment while ensuring that DHS's assessment approach is more consistent with the NIPP.

Response: Non-concur. DHS does not agree with this recommendation because:

- NPPD IP and other program officials and SMEs believe the existing NRE analysis by both Government and non-governmental entities has sufficiently characterized the risk environment;

- GAO's characterization of existing DHS GPS risk assessment work is inaccurate, particularly as relates to the incorporation of risk analysis best practices;

- GAO does not identify any key decisions that would benefit from additional analysis;

- The availability of more detailed data covering various risk factors associated with GPS has not improved since the development of DHS's NRE, and there is significant uncertainty as to when, or if, additional data will be available for additional analysis.

- Per Presidential Policy Directive -21, "Critical Infrastructure Security and Resilience," the NIPP is already being updated and indications are that no significant changes will be made to the risk assessment methodology; therefore, the current NRE will not need to be re-accomplished to meet updated criteria.

DHS requests that GAO consider this recommendation resolved and closed.

Recommendation 2: As part of current critical infrastructure planning with SSAs and sector partners, develop and issue a plan and metrics to measure the effectiveness of GPS risk mitigation efforts on critical infrastructure resiliency.

Response: Concur. As the coordinator of critical infrastructure at the federal level, NPPD IP will issue guidance to SSAs regarding the need to mitigate risks to GPS applications in the respective sector. As the SSAs coordinate activities in their sectors, each will be responsible for instituting programs and reporting outputs to IP in order for the latter to report on the overall national-level effort to mitigate risk associated with GPS. Estimated Completion Date (ECD): September 30, 2014.

GAO also recommended that the Secretaries of Transportation and Homeland Security:

Recommendation 3: Establish a formal, written agreement that details how the agencies plan to address their shared responsibility. This agreement should address uncertainties, including clarifying and defining DOT's and DHS's respective roles, responsibilities, and authorities; establishing clear, agreed-upon outcomes; establishing how the agencies will monitor and report on progress towards those outcomes; and setting forth the agencies' plans for examining relevant issues, such as the roles of the SSAs and industry, how NSPD-39 fits into the risk management framework, whether an update to NSPD-39 is needed, or other issues as deemed necessary by the agencies.

4

Response: Concur. DHS will coordinate with interagency partners to further efforts to institute National Security Presidential Directive (NSPD) 39 mandates, to include the NSPD-39 back-up capabilities requirement. DHS and the U.S. Department of Transportation (DOT) will establish a formal, written agreement that will clearly delineate roles and responsibilities with established outcomes; however, it is important to note that the ability to fully implement agreed-upon shared tasks will be contingent on the availability of personnel and financial resources. Relevant DHS program officials and SMEs will meet no later than December 31, 2013, to establish internal roles and responsibilities, then will reach out to interagency partners, including DOT, in 2014 to address interagency planning. ECD: September 30, 2014.

Again, thank you for the opportunity to review and provide comment on this draft report. Technical comments were previously provided under separate cover. Please feel free to contact me if you have any questions. We look forward to working with you in the future.

Sincerely,

Jim H. Crumpacker
Director
Departmental GAO-OIG Liaison Office

5

Appendix III: GAO Contact and Staff Acknowledgments

GAO Contacts	Mark Goldstein (202) 512-2834 or goldsteinm@gao.gov Joseph Kirschbaum (202) 512-9971 or kirschbaumj@gao.gov
Staff Acknowledgments	In addition to the individuals named above, Sally Moino and Glenn Davis, Assistant Directors; Eli Albagli; Melissa Bodeau; Katherine Davis; Richard Hung; Bert Japikse; SaraAnn Moessbauer; Josh Ormond; Nalylee Padilla; and Daniel Rodriguez made key contributions to this report.

GAO's Mission	The Government Accountability Office, the audit, evaluation, and investigative arm of Congress, exists to support Congress in meeting its constitutional responsibilities and to help improve the performance and accountability of the federal government for the American people. GAO examines the use of public funds; evaluates federal programs and policies; and provides analyses, recommendations, and other assistance to help Congress make informed oversight, policy, and funding decisions. GAO's commitment to good government is reflected in its core values of accountability, integrity, and reliability.
Obtaining Copies of GAO Reports and Testimony	The fastest and easiest way to obtain copies of GAO documents at no cost is through GAO's website (http://www.gao.gov). Each weekday afternoon, GAO posts on its website newly released reports, testimony, and correspondence. To have GAO e-mail you a list of newly posted products, go to http://www.gao.gov and select "E-mail Updates."
Order by Phone	The price of each GAO publication reflects GAO's actual cost of production and distribution and depends on the number of pages in the publication and whether the publication is printed in color or black and white. Pricing and ordering information is posted on GAO's website, http://www.gao.gov/ordering.htm. Place orders by calling (202) 512-6000, toll free (866) 801-7077, or TDD (202) 512-2537. Orders may be paid for using American Express, Discover Card, MasterCard, Visa, check, or money order. Call for additional information.
Connect with GAO	Connect with GAO on Facebook, Flickr, Twitter, and YouTube. Subscribe to our RSS Feeds or E-mail Updates. Listen to our Podcasts. Visit GAO on the web at www.gao.gov.
To Report Fraud, Waste, and Abuse in Federal Programs	Contact: Website: http://www.gao.gov/fraudnet/fraudnet.htm E-mail: fraudnet@gao.gov Automated answering system: (800) 424-5454 or (202) 512-7470
Congressional Relations	Katherine Siggerud, Managing Director, siggerudk@gao.gov, (202) 512-4400, U.S. Government Accountability Office, 441 G Street NW, Room 7125, Washington, DC 20548
Public Affairs	Chuck Young, Managing Director, youngc1@gao.gov, (202) 512-4800 U.S. Government Accountability Office, 441 G Street NW, Room 7149 Washington, DC 20548

www.ingramcontent.com/pod-product-compliance
Lightning Source LLC
Chambersburg PA
CBHW080546290526
45790CB00006B/2574